COURAGEOUS
PARENTING

COURAGEOUS
PARENTING

JACK & DEB
GRAHAM

CROSSWAY BOOKS

A PUBLISHING MINISTRY OF
GOOD NEWS PUBLISHERS
WHEATON, ILLINOIS

Courageous Parenting

Copyright © 2006 by Jack Graham

Published by Crossway Books
      A publishing ministry of Good News Publishers
      1300 Crescent Street
      Wheaton, Illinois 60187

Cover design: Josh Dennis

First printing, 2006

Printed in the United States of America

Unless otherwise indicated, Scripture quotations are taken from *The Holy Bible: English Standard Version*®. Copyright © 2001 by Crossway Bibles, a publishing ministry of Good News Publishers. Used by permission. All rights reserved.

Scripture quotations marked NKJV are taken from *The Holy Bible: The New King James Version*. Copyright © 1982 by Thomas Nelson, Inc. Used by permission.

Scripture quotations marked NLT are taken from *Holy Bible: New Living Translation,* copyright © 1996 by Tyndale Charitable Trust. Used by permission of Tyndale House Publishers.

Library of Congress Cataloging-in-Publication Data
Graham, Jack, 1950–
   Courageous parenting / Jack and Deb Graham.
     p. cm.
ISBN 13: 978-1-58134-744-9
ISBN 10: 1-58134-744-8 (hardcover : alk. paper)
   1. Parenting—Religious aspects—Christianity. 2. Child rearing—
Religious aspects—Christianity. I. Graham, Deb, 1951–   II. Title.
BV4529.G68   2006
248.8'45—dc22   2006014223

Q		16	15	14	13	12	11	10	09	08	07	06
15	14	13	12	11	10	9	8	7	6	5	4	3	2	1

To

IAN JAMES GRAHAM
our first grandchild

*With the prayer that your light will shine
into future generations with the love of Jesus.*

*You remind us that
"the generation of the upright will be blessed"
(Psalm 112:2)*

*We are blessed beyond measure in seeing
our children's children.*

CONTENTS

INTRODUCTION

BEFORE THERE WAS Dr. Phil or Baby Einstein, we became parents. Sometimes we wonder how we made it! We didn't have disposable diapers or bibs, and our children didn't have video games or computers in those early years. But what we had was each other and the Lord, and what our kids had mostly was us. There's no doubt that we made hundreds of mistakes. It's a good thing we didn't know about all of them then or we might not have made it through our children's teenage years.

We gave our children all we could. They never went hungry or barefooted (except for the one born in Florida), and they were never mistreated. Yet they did not have the advantages today's infants have. We marvel at the innovative products that our son and daughter-in-love have at their fingertips for our grandson Ian. There is a toy, device, or instructional aid for every minute of a child's life. Sometimes we need an instruction manual just to get all of these gadgets to work.

As wonderful as all these things are, the age-old questions of parenting are still being asked. How do you raise a child to become a well-rounded, successful adult? How do you keep from making so many mistakes? How do you train your children to love God? Generations of parents have prepared, planned, and toiled, only to feel insecure, lost, and helpless at times.

We will be the first to tell you that we didn't do it all right. But in the same breath we can say it wasn't because we didn't try. In fact, we are still trying today. Although our "baby" graduated from college while we were writing this book, we still have a lifetime of parenting ahead of us.

With each new age, parents shuffle and realign their parenting skills and attitude. That's important because being a parent is a lifetime calling.

Parenting is a journey through time. It has hills and valleys, but the road extends beyond our limited eyesight. God is gracious to only give us what we have the ability to comprehend now, but day after day He reveals to us His plan for our lives and for the lives of our children.

In addition to the three children God gave us to raise, He also gave us two who never were ours to hold. But because we lost these two children during pregnancy, we especially loved, appreciated, enjoyed, and cherished the children the Lord put in our arms. "The fruit of the womb" is truly God's "reward" (Psalm 127:3).

May God give you the desires of your heart concerning your family. And as He blesses you, may you live each day with renewed determination to be courageous parents.

Jack and Deb Graham

ACKNOWLEDGMENTS

TO CROSSWAY BOOKS, for their support and belief in our message. We do not take lightly the confidence you place in us.

To Phil Rawley, our friend and editor who walks the path with us and molds our words into shape; and to Philip, his son and writing partner, who also made valuable contributions to the book.

To Jason, Toby, Kelly, and Josh Graham. You are the reason we still try to understand God's parenting plan for our lives.

To Bob and Joan Frost, who faithfully pray for our family and are grandparents deluxe.

To the memory of Tom and Emogene Graham, and to Doyle Peters, who parented us to love God and each other.

PART ONE

A BIBLICAL PLAN
FOR THE FAMILY

1

IT TAKES THREE TO MAKE PARENTING WORK

ACCORDING TO A FAMOUS QUOTE attributed to Abraham Lincoln, "You can fool some of the people all of the time, and all of the people some of the time, but you can not fool all of the people all of the time."

With apologies to Mr. Lincoln, we want to edit his statement into this important word to fellow parents: "You can fool some of your children all of the time, and all of your children some of the time, but you can't fool all of your children all of the time."

In other words, the only way to make parenting work the way God intended is to keep it real! Our desire in this book is to help you accomplish this in two major ways: first and foremost, by sharing what God's Word has to say about the demanding and immensely rewarding task of being a parent; and second, by sharing the successes, mistakes, and observations we have accumulated along the way in this wonderful, and often frightening, task of parenthood. We promise to share our hearts with you at the most real and transparent level we can achieve.

We are not experts, but we have learned some things from being parents and serving in the pastorate for well over thirty years. We've seen the good, the bad, and the ugly when it comes to the home and family. This includes many wonderful and successful marriages and families, from whom we have learned valuable and positive lessons. And we have observed many families in trouble. So we know something of the downside as well as the upside of parenting.

We were married on May 22, 1970 and have raised three children. (We offered to include a fold-out section of photos of our grandson in the book, but the publisher politely declined!) We made a commitment early on to apply biblical principles in our marriage and childrearing, and God has blessed us incredibly. Our two sons and our daughter love the Lord and are serving Him faithfully. We can say with the apostle John, "I have no greater joy than to hear that my children are walking in the truth" (3 John 4).

Becoming a parent is relatively easy. It doesn't require any prior education, qualifications, skills, or experience—or even the cost of a marriage license in some cases. But there is a huge difference between *becoming* a parent and successfully *parenting* the child we have brought into the world.

Here is our bottom-line conviction and the basic premise of this book: God designed the task of bearing and raising children to be accomplished in the power of His Holy Spirit within the bonds of a faithful, loving, lifelong marriage. This has to be the place to start, even though it is obvious that many marriages do not last a lifetime. Trying to be a marital partner and parent without understanding God's intention is like trying to cut a photograph to fit a frame without knowing the dimensions of the frame.

If you are reading this book as a single parent, we want to encourage you in your difficult task. But regardless of your current marital status, if you are a Christian, the power of the Holy Spirit is available daily to help you raise your children "in the discipline and instruction of the Lord" (Ephesians 6:4).

This goal is within the reach of every parent or prospective parent—regardless of background, education level, social status, or economic condition. This truth should give all of us hope that we can be successful parents and raise children who become mature, responsible adults and committed followers of Jesus Christ.

One wag said, "Love at first sight is nothing special. It's when two people have been looking at each other for years that it becomes a miracle." Well, we have been looking at each other for over thirty-five years now, and it is still getting better and better. We like what we see in each other because of the Lord's presence in our lives and marriage. He is the One who has enabled us to build our marriage and family on the fundamentals of His Word.

Every winning team in any sport majors on the fundamentals of the game. They keep going back to the basics. They go to training camp every year, even if they won it all the season before, because you never outgrow your need of the basics. These are the things we want to present in this book.

A GREAT MARRIAGE REQUIRES THREE PEOPLE

It is highly unlikely that a husband and wife who are unhappy and completely at odds in their marriage, or are indifferent and content to let their marriage deteriorate, can then turn around and become an effective set of parents doing a dynamic job of raising their children. Family life doesn't work that way. So we want to begin where God's Word begins, with a man and a woman coming together to form a marriage and a family.

God Himself performed the first marriage, as recorded in Genesis 2:22. The Bible says, "And the rib that the LORD God had taken from the man he made into a woman and brought her to the man." Then God blessed the union of Adam and Eve: "Therefore a man shall leave his father and his mother and hold fast to his wife, and they shall become one flesh" (v. 24).

This was not simply the first marriage ceremony, but a picture of the three people it takes to make a great marriage. Two people become one flesh in marriage, but then those two people also become one spiritually when they are joined in spirit to God in the Person of Jesus Christ. He is the third Person at the center of a great marriage.

A Biblical Plan for the Family

Jack: Guys, let's get real for a minute. Many men spend more time working on their golf game, hobby, or profession than they do working on their marriages. But marriage is not a 50-50 arrangement in which all you have to do is kick in your half of the deal. Marriage demands a 100 percent commitment from both spouses. And since God wired women to be responders, when you give all of yourself to your wife, she is going to respond in kind, and you will begin to enjoy a fulfillment in your marriage you never thought possible!

But it starts with you, because you are the thermostat that regulates the temperature in your marriage. Your wife is the thermometer that records and reflects either the warmth or the frigid conditions in your home.

Marriage Is God's Idea from the Beginning

Let's not forget who invented marriage and the family. This was God's idea! Therefore marriage is not a human contract that can be broken at will but a divine covenant established by God to be supreme over all other earthly relationships and complete in its commitment. And since God created marriage, He has given us the "manual" to make it work in the pages of His Word.

We can even find helpful marriage principles in the most unlikely places in the Bible, as in these verses from the Old Testament:

> *Two are better than one, because they have a good reward for their toil. For if they fall, one will lift up his fellow. But woe to him who is alone when he falls and has not another to lift him up! Again, if two lie together, they keep warm, but how can one keep warm alone? And though a man might prevail against one who is alone, two will withstand him—a threefold cord is not quickly broken. (Ecclesiastes 4:9-12)*

Here is the cord that can tie married life together and keep it strong even when the world tries to topple it. Those three cords are you, your mate, and the Lord Jesus Christ.

18

God Wants to Be Part of Your Marriage

Please don't misunderstand. Simply being Christians by itself does not guarantee that a man and woman will have a happy marriage. Perhaps you heard about the pastor who went to a fourth-grade class to talk to the children about home and family. At one point the pastor asked those nine-year-olds, "Can any of you tell me what God says about marriage?"

There was a long, quiet pause before a little boy raised his hand. "All right, son," the pastor said. "Tell us what God says about marriage."

The little boy responded, "Father, forgive them, for they know not what they do!"

We have to admit there are too many marriages even between Christians in which one or both partners would echo that little boy's honest reaction. Someone has said that marriage is like a three ring circus: there is the engagement ring, the wedding ring, and suffer-ring. It's possible even for believers to have a three-ring circus marriage. But God's ideal and will is a "threefold cord" marriage in which Christ is the center and heart of the relationship.

God Put His Blessing on the Marriage Union

A marriage like this is possible in Christ! You can't spend enough money to buy it, which is good news for most of us. J. Paul Getty, who was one of the richest men in the world, once said, "I would give my entire fortune for one happy marriage."

But great marriages are not built on fortunes. They are built on the blessing of God when two people bind themselves to Him as they bind themselves to each other. Outside of a person's relationship with Christ, there is nothing on earth more precious and valuable than the relationship between a husband and wife.

Remember, it was God who blessed the first union between a man and a woman. Again, the Bible says of Adam and Eve:

So God created man in his own image, in the image of God he created him; male and female he created them. And God blessed them. *And*

A Biblical Plan for the Family

God said to them, "Be fruitful and multiply and fill the earth and sub-
due it and have dominion over the fish of the sea and over the birds of
the heavens and over every living thing that moves on the earth."
(Genesis 1:27-28, emphasis added)

The blessing that God built into marriage is not only evident in the spiritual realm but in the physical as well. Research has now shown that a strong and happy marriage is profitable emotionally and physically. For instance, we now know that married people live longer than unmarried people and report a higher degree of happiness and satisfaction in life. They also go to doctors less often and make less use of health care services.

Someone even researched mortality records dating back to the nineteenth century and found that the highest suicide rates occurred among the divorced, followed by the widowed and the never-married, while the lowest rates of suicide were among married couples.

We could cite many examples that agree with these findings, both on the positive and negative side. Many of us had a front-row seat and watched first in awe and then in sadness as the famous marriage between Britain's Prince Charles and Lady Diana unraveled in front of the world.

Literally the whole world watched as these two were united in a storybook royal wedding in 1981. The pomp and circumstance were incredible. It was a never-to-be-forgotten wedding.

But the royal marriage itself was another story. It soon became little more than fodder for the tabloids and then ended in tragedy when Diana was killed in a car accident.

God Wants Us to Work at Our Marriages

Sometimes people say, "I believe our marriage was made in heaven." Whether that's true or not, one thing is sure. Marriages are worked out on earth—and it takes a lot of work to make a marriage work. When some people's marriages start to go sour, instead of working on the relationship they say, "Well, I guess I missed it on this one. Maybe God will bless my next marriage."

That kind of thinking is not only unbiblical but ignores the truth that

20

marriage is a day-to-day growth process between two people who are committed to stay at it and enjoy the immense rewards of a fulfilling marriage. Our salvation is free, the gift of God to us (Ephesians 2:8-9), but a great marriage comes at the price of diligent work.

Here's something to think about in that regard. The apostle Paul wrote: "Work out your own salvation with fear and trembling" (Philippians 2:12). We just said that salvation is free to us. But even this marvelous grace-gift has to be worked out—nurtured, cultivated, given careful attention—as we apply it to our lives on a daily basis.

And notice that Paul told us to work out our salvation "with fear and trembling." That's a reminder that the great salvation God purchased for us at the cost of His dear Son's blood is not something to treat casually or take lightly, like a stroll in the park.

So here's a logical question. If something as divine and supernatural as the gift of salvation—something definitely made in heaven—needs to be worked out, how much more does the gift of marriage need to be worked out? The answer suggests itself! Marriage is God's gift to us, and our diligence to make a home and family that brings Him glory is our gift back to God.

God Supplies the Power That Makes Marriage Work

The reason we can make marriage work is that we are not working alone. Paul provided this truth as he continued in Philippians 2: "For it is God who works in you, both to will and to work for his good pleasure" (v. 13). The apostle was speaking of our salvation, but the principle applies to marriage. It is God's will that marriage be lifelong. Jesus said, "What therefore God has joined together, let not man separate" (Matthew 19:6). God will supply His power to those who seek Him. But without this, our efforts won't get us anywhere.

This is why it is so important to understand that marriage is truly a threefold cord. Solomon was not just being poetic in Ecclesiastes 4. Without the third cord, the Lord Jesus Christ, to bind a relationship together, it can quickly unravel as a married couple starts using the "D" word.

Divorce Doesn't Solve Anyone's Problems

Divorce has become a tragedy of epic proportions in our culture. We're living in a time when more and more people throw away their marriages with the idea that they'll start over with someone else. And perhaps most tragic of all, this idea that marriage is disposable has crept into the church. Divorce statistics for Christians have caught up with those of the secular world, and there seems to be no letup in this trend.

Jack: The Bible says that God hates divorce (Malachi 2:16). Yes, there are certain very restricted cases of unfaithfulness where divorce is permitted. But it is not commanded. Our culture seems to love divorce. People view divorce much like they view abortion—as a way to escape the consequences of their choices.

But divorce doesn't solve anyone's problem. My experience as a pastor is that most marriages are abandoned for no good reason, by which I mean for no *biblical* reason. I have seen far too many marriages end in divorce that could have been saved. Most marriages that fail do so because of a lack of obedience to God and a lack of commitment to one another.

Even adultery does not have to be a cause of divorce if the guilty party repents and is forgiven, and if the marriage partners earnestly seek restoration and the rekindling of their love. Biblical love is an act of the will, a matter of obedience to God, which is why the Bible can command us to love one another.

Deb: We hear people say, "I just fell in love." This is often the romantic ideal presented to girls and young women by music, movies, and popular culture in general. There is no denying that two people may feel attracted to each other even at their first meeting, but that is not love. You don't fall in love the way you fall over a chair or fall into a hole, suddenly and without warning. People speak of love as if it is such a strong emotion there is nothing we can do about it once it takes hold of us. Love certainly involves the emotions, but at heart it is a commitment of our will to seek the other person's best interest at any cost.

Marriage is a lot like a mirror. When you see yourself in a mirror and realize you need some work, that's not the time to break the mirror and walk away. Marriage is a very accurate mirror of what is really happening in a person's life. So if your "marriage mirror" reveals some things that need attention, don't break the marriage and walk away. That's the time to deal with the problems—to get back to the fundamentals of God's Word.

We're Losing Our Families

The importance of getting marriage right reaches far beyond the four walls of our houses. The breakdown of the God-ordained institution of marriage should be a serious concern to all of us, because as we look around it is obvious that we're losing our families. And as the family goes, so goes the entire culture. It doesn't matter how much the social engineers talk about a new paradigm of the family. None of the unusual, or even bizarre, "family" arrangements we see today can replace God's plan for one man and one woman to raise their own children in the context of a loving, committed marriage and nurturing home.

Jack: I will never forget the day one of the ministers at our church broke down and wept at a staff meeting. He works with young marrieds and was telling about several couples with problems who were talking about divorce after just a few years or even months of marriage. This man has a tender heart, and it was breaking as he saw these couples drifting apart. We prayed as a staff that God would do a mighty work in their lives to heal their marriages and keep them from breaking their covenant.

Let me say again that marriage is not a human contract but a covenant—a promise—made before God. Human contracts can be altered or nullified, but the promise that marriage partners make is "for as long as [they] both shall live."

The statistics on family breakdown are startling. One million children a year in America are negatively influenced by divorce. The divorce rate has gone up so astronomically that the numbers are staggering. At the beginning of the twentieth century, the divorce rate was about 12 percent. Now it's up to around 50 percent—half of all marriages.

GOD CAN RESTORE A MARRIAGE

So how do we go about restoring marriages and rebuilding homes? The same way we would eat an elephant, one bite at a time. It has to be done one marriage, one family, one victory at a time. Rather than accept things as they are, we can move forward to things as they ought to be because God can restore any marriage that has been torn by conflict or withered from neglect.

Many Christian homes used to have a little plaque or cross-stitch on the wall with this declaration of faith: "As for me and my house, we will serve the LORD" (Joshua 24:15). We baby boomers and Gen-Xers don't hang slogans like this on our walls anymore, but maybe we should! What a wonderful daily reminder of the commitment God wants and expects from us. If each of us, one couple at a time, will take a stand for the Lord, we can gnaw away at the "elephant" of divorce and family breakdown.

During the early days of World War II, as England was being besieged by Nazi air raids, many of the people were ready to abandon their homeland. That's when British leader Sir Winston Churchill is said to have declared, "Victory is not won by evacuation!" And the people stood their ground. We want to make the same statement about marriage. Victory is not won by evacuation—by abandoning our commitments, giving up, quitting—but by persevering by the grace and power of God.

When All Else Fails, Read the Directions

A soldier who begins a march on the wrong foot will be out of step the entire way unless he recognizes his mistake and makes a conscious effort to shift his feet so he can follow the drill sergeant's marching orders.

One problem with many marriages is that they get started on the wrong foot. That is, many couples don't really understand the purpose for which God created marriage. So they get married for all the wrong reasons—for sex, money, or status, to fulfill an infatuation, or perhaps worst of all, because everyone else was getting married and it seemed like the thing to do at the time.

Marrying for the wrong reasons is bad, but the good news is that even couples who started their marriage on the wrong foot can pull it together. Because God is the Restorer of marriages, these couples can have wonderfully satisfying, God-honoring marriages and can become great parents.

Actually, all of us need to be reminded what marriage is really about, which is why it helps to go back and read the directions in God's Word. In Genesis 2 we learn why God created Eve and brought her to Adam.

The order of events in this chapter is very interesting because God wanted to teach Adam his need for someone else. So after announcing, "It is not good that the man should be alone; I will make him a helper fit for [or, comparable to] him" (v. 18), the next thing God did was not to create Eve, as we might expect, but to create the animals and bring them to Adam so he could name them.

God did this to show Adam that He had provided a mate for every animal. And as Adam named each one, he also learned that none of the animals was his type. He named everything from the aardvarks to the zebras but did not find "a helper fit for him" (v. 20). And even though Adam had a good life in a perfect environment, he suddenly realized something was missing. He felt alone for the first time.

God already knew that Adam's aloneness was "not good." But it wasn't until *Adam* realized it that he was ready for Eve. That's when God fashioned Eve from Adam's rib and united the two in marriage with this instruction: "Therefore a man shall leave his father and his mother and hold fast to [or cleave to] his wife, and they shall become one flesh" (v. 24).

The foundational purpose of marriage is that both the man and the woman find their completion in one another, so that together they can fulfill God's design for their lives. When the Bible describes Eve as "fit for" or "comparable to" Adam, it means she corresponded to him. Adam was incomplete without Eve. He needed a helper to complete him and to complete the human race. Woman was created to be man's completer, not his competer.

We noted above that the verb "hold fast to" in Genesis 2:24 can also mean "cleave," as it is translated in the King James Version. This is a great word that means "to cling to, to stick to" like glue. Jesus even quoted Genesis 2:24 when He warned us not to try and tear apart a marriage that God has glued together (Matthew 19:5-6).

Eve was the cure for Adam's aloneness and incompleteness. The two of them were like two pieces of a puzzle that fit together perfectly and completed the picture of marriage.

Put Your Marriage Before All Other Relationships

Giving marriage its proper place in our relationships is a challenge we face today that Adam and Eve didn't have to deal with—at least not at first. Marriage changes every other human relationship. Some previous ties are severed, and others are moved down a notch on the priority list because a new Number One is in town.

This seems so patently obvious that some may wonder why we even mention it. But we all know there's nothing automatic about this process. God knew it too, which is why He told the man to "leave his father and his mother" in Genesis 2:24 before He told him to cleave to his wife. Some couples spend a lifetime trying to get the leaving part right.

As both parents and parents-in-law, we know how hard it is to cut those parental strings. But we also understand from our own experience, as well as from Scripture, how important it is for young couples to leave their homes and establish a home of their own.

We were just kids when we got married while in college. Our parents helped us with our school bills, but we were committed to make it on our own. Sometimes young couples decide they will move in with Mom and Dad until they get on their feet. But that can be a conflict waiting to happen. There's a reason they make television sitcoms out of arrangements like that! It can be very funny on the screen, but very unfunny in real life. No one has ever improved on God's plan.

Friends can also be a challenge. Some men marry with the mentality that they are just adding one more buddy to their group—a nice addition to the gang who's prettier and smells better than the rest! A new husband will often be teased by his single friends about being "out of commission" or "ball-and-chained" because he doesn't hang out with them as much anymore.

But the jokes and teasing can't obscure the fact that a husband who understands God's design for marriage knows that his wife is his new best friend as well as his life partner. It works the other way too. Today's women generally have a much wider circle of friends and acquaintances than their grandmothers had because most modern-day women live in much larger communities and also work outside the home. Those relationships also have to be subordinated to the marriage partnership.

A friend told us about a young family that once lived next to him in the Dallas area. The couple began having problems, and it wasn't long before the husband left. During this time the wife almost nonchalantly told my friend that the women she worked with were encouraging her to divorce her husband, telling her she didn't have to put up with him. They even offered to help her find a divorce attorney who could make sure she got a good settlement. Unfortunately, she made it clear to our friend that she was taking their advice, and this couple eventually divorced.

Now to be sure, there were serious problems in that home. But this illustrates the undue influence friends can have if these relationships are allowed to supersede the marriage bond. Thankfully, many of us can also point to godly friends who are a great example, encouragement, and blessing.

Don't get us wrong. It's great to have friends. But marriage is sort of like it was when we were kids. Remember how you could have lots of friends but only one best friend? And you had to let that other kid know he or she was your best friend so he or she wouldn't become someone else's best friend. And you had to stick with each other, at least until one of you changed his or her mind.

Well, husbands and wives have a one-and-only best friend in each other. And they need to stick with each other. Being best friends as well as lovers is a great way to build a marriage. It's one thing to divorce a spouse, but it's much harder to divorce your best friend.

Put Another Log on the Fire and Fan the Flames

As husbands and wives we need to ask ourselves, "Am I doing whatever it takes to strengthen my relationship with my mate? Am I engaging in any attitude or action that is detrimental to my marriage? Is there anything in my life that's driving us apart rather than bringing us together?"

The fire of love and commitment in your marriage may be burning low right now, but it can be rekindled in Jesus Christ. Just because the flames in a fireplace have died down to glowing embers doesn't mean the fire is out. Just put a fresh log on those embers, fan them a little, and the flames will rise.

Your marriage can burn brightly when you commit your lives to Jesus Christ and then determine to rekindle the love and devotion you once enjoyed in your marriage. Great parents are prepared and nurtured in great marriages!

2

THE LOVING LEADERSHIP OF A HUSBAND AND FATHER

WE MENTIONED IN THE previous chapter that a wife and mother in a home is like a thermometer, sensing and reflecting the home's temperature. But a father and husband is like a home's thermostat, which determines and regulates the temperature.

That is a helpful analogy to understand how each partner in a marriage and each parent in a family is designed to function. A man has a lot to do with how warm or how chilly his marriage is and whether there is a numbing coldness or a glowing warmth around the table when the family sits down together.

This may be news to many men because qualities like warmth and intimacy are usually considered to be a woman's specialty. We're not saying a man has to "get in touch with his feminine side" to be successful in his home. But there is no question that the Word of God places the primary responsibility for a family's welfare on the husband and father in that home. Dad, you won't find any better "thermostat settings" to set the right temperature in your marriage and family than these two biblical admonitions: "Husbands, love your wives, as Christ loved the church and gave himself up for her," and "Fathers, do not provoke your children to anger, but bring them up in the discipline and instruction of the Lord" (Ephesians 5:25; 6:4).

It takes only a few seconds to read those verses but a lifetime to live them out. In this chapter we want to help husbands understand more clearly what it means to love their wives with Christ-like love and give men some practical ways to do this and then help fathers with the awesome task of raising their children to know and love and follow the Lord. These two roles are intimately connected; so talking about the one necessarily involves the other.

You've probably heard the old saying that the best thing a father can do for his children is to love their mother. The reason that saying is still around is that it has the ring of truth to it. Most of us could count on one hand the number of couples we have known whose marriages were in disarray but who were doing a dynamite job of parenting and the kids showed absolutely no effect from their parents' marriage woes. It seldom works that way.

One challenge in writing a book on subjects such as marriage or parenting—or maybe we should say, one challenge in getting men to read books on these subjects—is that many men feel intimidated or defeated in these areas before they even begin. Men often say things like, "I'm just not very good at this relationship thing," or "I kind of leave the stuff at home to my wife because she's so much better at it than I am."

The problem with this approach is, that's not how God has wired marriage and family relationships to work. Many women *are* better at relationships than men. And it's generally true that nurturing and all that goes with it comes more naturally to women than it does to men. But part of the reason is that most women work a lot harder at relationships and take them more seriously than men. So instead of using their shortcomings as an excuse to opt out of their God-given roles, men need to realize that they will have to give these areas more attention. And having a wife beside him who is good at relationships can be a tremendous help to a man if he will watch and listen and learn from her example.

So when it's all said and done in this area of home and family, we're left with the biblical model of a father and husband who is a loving servant-leader to his wife and a guide and instructor to his children. The good news is that men can not only improve in this "relationship thing," they can become excellent fathers and husbands who are true role models of what it means to love, cherish, nurture, and teach their families.

Jack: Men, there's simply no way around it. The leadership of our homes and families rests with us. We are called to follow Christ in our lives and to be God's man for our wives and children. And I want to encourage you that you *can* do it. There is not one truth or principle from God's Word you will read here that is beyond your ability to learn and apply in your home with the Holy Spirit's help. Courageous parenting is really Holy Spirit parenting.

The Holy Spirit's role in marriage and parenting is critical because Ephesians 5:22—6:4, the apostle Paul's classic treatment of marriage and family relationships, is founded on and flows out of this fundamental command: "Do not get drunk with wine, for that is debauchery, but be filled with the Spirit" (5:18). This filling is the control of the Spirit, our yielding to His will and direction so completely that we begin to exhibit the characteristics of Christ the way a person with too much alcohol in him exhibits the characteristics of a drunk.

The verses that follow tell us what the Spirit-filled life looks like in the church (5:19-21) and then in the family (5:22—6:4). In the next chapter we'll deal with Paul's word to wives, but most of the ink in Ephesians 5:22-33 is given to men, first as husbands and then as fathers.

Deb: One of the greatest influences on my life was my father, who played such an important role in our family. I can recall early in life being taken to church. But most of my early recollections were of my mother's involvement at church in mission organizations and Bible study functions. Then at the age of eight I saw my father walk the aisle of our small

Texas church to accept Jesus as his Savior, and he became a different person. He became very involved in teaching a teenage boys' Bible study class. He also volunteered in the church's bus outreach ministry.

My father was a rural mail carrier by vocation but a true minister by calling. Although he never preached a sermon, he preached volumes to me. A man of great knowledge and skill, he was a private math tutor for advanced high school students in our school district. Young men and women were in and out of our home night after night seeking his insight into calculus and trigonometry. But more importantly, they were receiving a huge dose of support from a father figure who cared about them both educationally and spiritually. What they paid for by the hour I received free every day.

By the time I was in high school my father gave freely of his time to tutor any student who attended our church. He would leave his job every Wednesday and go straight to the church to hold a tutoring class in whatever type of math was needed. As soon as he finished tutoring he would take his turn at helping with the evening fellowship meal. He was our pastor's greatest supporter, most loyal friend, and most faithful prayer partner.

When I left for college, my father was my constant supporter. He wrote letters, called me, and always reminded me of what I could do with my life. He set the standard by which I would choose a mate; and when I met Jack, I knew I had found that man.

As sometimes is the case, God allows suffering to be part of our lives. Jack and I had only been married a short time when my father was diagnosed with melanoma cancer. In a matter of months he was on his deathbed.

For days he lay in that hospital bed singing and teaching his teenage boys a Bible lesson he had recently prepared. That lesson dealt with heaven. What Dad had poured into his heart had saturated his mind, and in those final moments on earth he spoke of the only real thing he knew—that he would soon be in the presence of the Lord who had given him life and meaning. In forty-odd years he had found the meaning of life, and he shared it until that wintry morning he went to be with his

Savior and experienced all that he had taught those boys about his new home.

The influence my father had on my life still reveals itself to me each day. In the summer of 1989, Jack and I were living in West Palm Beach, Florida. We had been serving there for over eight years among a wonderful congregation of believers. We fully expected we would be there for the rest of our lives. Little did we know that God had other plans. Thousands of miles away in a hurting and broken church in North Dallas, a committee met to pray that God would lead them to a man who would come and lead their church. By all human measures we were not the candidates for the position.

But little did we know that my father's faithful service would be a factor in that committee's decision to call us to that pulpit. The committee had one member who was once in my father's Bible study class. In a committee meeting where Jack's name came up, this man realized who I was. Our name was no longer a name on a list but a reminder of the spiritual influence that my father formerly had in this man's life.

You see, Dad had kept in touch with this former class member even years after this young man had graduated and gone to Vietnam. My father prayed for him and wrote him letters of encouragement during that time. As a direct result of Dad's spiritual influence, Jack and I were called to serve Prestonwood Baptist Church.

The legacy my father left me is one I cherish greatly. He represented my heavenly Father during those formative years. My appreciation and respect for what God has done in my life come from seeing a life totally and completely dedicated to His service—that of my father.

LOVE YOUR WIFE IN A WAY THAT WILL MAKE YOUR MARRIAGE EXCITING

It's worth quoting Ephesians 5:25 again: "Husbands, love your wives, as Christ loved the church and gave himself up for her."

Love your wife. These three words describe a husband's principal responsibility in his marriage. Husband, love your wife because you set the temperature for your home. God designed a man to be the leader and initiator at home, and as his wife and children respond to the loving, faithful leadership of a man who is committed to Christ and committed to them, that home will be an exciting place to live.

The love the Bible is talking about here is the highest form of love—*agape* love, the self-giving love of Christ that took Him to the cross for us. In Jesus we have the perfect example of the kind of love that husbands are to show to their wives. For men, being a great parent begins with "Love your wives." So here are five ways that men can express Christ-like love.

Love Your Wife with Passion

Using the word *passion* often suggests the sexual side of love. That's certainly a component of passion, and one expression of it. But we're using *passion* in the broader sense of a deep-seated love that begins in the heart and radiates out from there. Maybe a good synonym would be sacrificial love, which gets right to the core of what the Bible means by true love. Because Jesus loved the church, He "gave himself up for her," as we read above. He died for the church!

Deb: A lot of men would jump in here and say, "Hey, I'd be willing to throw myself in front of a Mack truck for my wife!" We wives appreciate that commitment, although we hope it never comes to that! But I think many other wives would join me in saying that a woman knows her husband loves her passionately when she sees him dying to himself in small ways each day—giving up his ego and his plans and his ambitions when necessary to put his wife first.

I suspect a lot of women would respond to their husbands' vow to die for them by saying, "I have no doubt my husband would take a bullet for me. I just wish he'd take a walk with me once in a while or take time to do something else I'd really enjoy doing." If you want a passionate wife, let her know she's Number One in your passions.

Love Your Wife with Purity

When we think of the purity of a husband's love for his wife, sexual purity in marriage is high on the list. The Bible says, "Let marriage be held in honor among all, and let the marriage bed be undefiled, for God will judge the sexually immoral and adulterous" (Hebrews 13:4).

But again, purity goes beyond the physical realm of marriage. Paul wrote in Ephesians 5 that Christ's love for the church included this purpose: "that he might sanctify her, having cleansed her by the washing of water with the word, so that he might present the church to himself in splendor, without spot or wrinkle or any such thing, that she might be holy and without blemish" (vv. 26-27).

We can read this and agree that we don't have any problem understanding how Jesus Christ is able to purify His bride by His love as He shed His blood for our sins. But how in the world can imperfect husbands show a sanctifying and cleansing love toward their wives? Is it even possible?

Well, it must be because it is part of God's will for every Christian husband. Consider the meaning of the word *pure*. At its most basic level, it means unadulterated or unmixed. A man can love his wife purely by loving her unconditionally, with no hidden or mixed motives. No husband does this perfectly, and no wife does either, because we are sinful people. But a man can strive to give his wife a pure, unmixed love that seeks the best for her regardless of the cost or response.

A husband can also keep his love pure by keeping the vows he made to his wife. This is committed love, the kind that says, "I promised to love and be faithful to you the day we were married, and I intend to do that for the rest of my life."

Love Your Wife with Purpose

Here's a third way a husband can love his wife. Loving with a purpose has to do with the goal of the sanctifying and cleansing love Paul spoke about in Ephesians 5:26-27. A husband who loves his wife the way Christ loves the church will lead her into a deeper, cleansing, and purifying relationship with Christ. It's true that all of us are responsible to develop our personal walk with the Lord. But a believing husband is called by God to act as the priest in his home, and in that role he can exhibit the kind of godly behavior and love that sets the example for his wife and children. In that sense a husband can be his wife's sanctifier. Husbands have the assignment from God to lead their wives to know and love and follow Jesus Christ and to present their brides to Christ with all of His beauty and love shining through them.

There can be a problem here because so many men are hesitant even to pray with their wives. It could be that men are afraid to open up to their wives, to share their hearts and their spiritual victories and defeats with them. But the best place to learn how to walk with the Lord is in your own home. That can be the most challenging place to start, but until our Christianity works at home we can't take it into the community.

Love Your Wife with Protection

A husband's first priority in relation to his wife is to make sure that he is doing his part to help her become properly related to God in a growing relationship. And he needs to add to this a sense of security in which his wife feels protected, understood, and cared for.

This kind of protection requires sensitivity on a husband's part. Peter addressed that in another classic passage on marriage that he concluded this way: "Likewise, husbands, live with your wives in an understanding way, showing honor to the woman as the weaker vessel, since they are heirs *with you* of the grace of life, so that your prayers may not be hindered" (1 Peter 3:7).

"The weaker vessel" does not mean an inferior vessel but a more precious one. It's the difference between the dishes you use every day and the fine china you get out when company comes. A woman is like expensive china that requires careful handling.

Jack: Deb made better grades in school than I did. My grades went up when I married her! Most of us men would readily admit that we married way over our heads. Deb has qualities, skills, and personality attributes that I could never muster up on my own. But one thing I can give her is the sense of security that all women seek and need. A wife needs to know that her husband is not only protecting her from physical harm but is creating a secure relationship emotionally and even materially in which she is free to be herself and to respond in love because she feels safe within her husband's love.

Love Your Wife with Provision

Wired into a man's makeup is the need to feel that he is able to provide for his family's needs by the work he does. This issue of work and income and who's the breadwinner in a home has become very complicated in today's culture. But regardless of whether both spouses work or who brings home the bigger paycheck, there are things a husband can provide for his wife that she not only needs but needs to get *from him*.

We've already suggested some of these, such as a sense of being loved and valued beyond anyone or anything else on earth. If you want a list of blessings you can provide for your mate, read 1 Corinthians 13 and determine that your love will be patient, kind, without pride or envy, and so forth.

Jack: Guys, we really have to work on this one! To love our wives passionately, purely, and purposefully, providing them with the protection and provision they need, is a lifetime assignment—and the most fulfilling thing we'll ever do.

I admit that it's not natural for us to love like this. But that's the point. It takes *supernatural* love for a man to love like this. That's why it is important to remember that the command for husbands to love their wives was written in the context of the Spirit-filled life. I can't love Deb like this in my own strength, but the Spirit of God can manifest the love of Christ through me to her.

LEAD YOUR WIFE IN A WAY THAT WILL MAKE YOUR HOME A POWERHOUSE FOR CHRIST

One of the debates that has been making the rounds in our culture for some time now is where, or even *if*, a father is supposed to fit into the family portrait. Our parents would have laughed at the idea that you can have children without a man being present for the process, but that's exactly what medical technology has made possible today.

A lot of nonsense has been dished out on this issue of whether "father knows best" or whether "father knows anything at all"! Much of the so-called expert opinion has come down on the side of saying that fathers are superfluous at best, if not completely unnecessary. But the only opinion that truly matters is God's, and His Word speaks powerfully about a father's incredible, irreplaceable influence on his children.

Don't Frustrate Your Children

We said at the outset that a man determines the temperature in his home, and we cited Ephesians 6:4 as a great setting for his role as a father: "Fathers, do not provoke your children to anger, but bring them up in the discipline and instruction of the Lord."

Another way to translate "provoke . . . to anger" is "to exasperate." We all know what it feels like to be exasperated or frustrated by another person. It's the feeling that nothing we do can please the one who is exasperating us. It usually leads the frustrated person to throw up his or her hands and say, "What's the use?" A corollary verse to Ephesians 6:4 brings this out: "Fathers, do not provoke your children, lest they become discouraged" (Colossians 3:21).

What are some things that exasperate children? One of the biggies is not letting them try things themselves and learn from their own mistakes.

A mother walked into the living room one day and found Junior watching television. "I thought you and your dad were in the garage working on your science project," she said.

Junior rolled his eyes, heaved a deep sigh, and gave his mother a knowing look as he said, "We are."

Mom got the picture. Dad had taken over because Junior wasn't doing it right or for whatever other reason, and Junior got the message that he wasn't needed. Dad hadn't even noticed when his son left the garage.

Of course, there are other child exasperators too. Applying correction without giving a reason or any affirmation leaves a child wondering what he did wrong and if he really is as bad as he seems to be at the moment. Another item on this list is a dad who doesn't live what he preaches—or in preacher terms, a dad whose possession doesn't live up to his profession. This one doesn't need a lot of elaboration. If our Christian lives as parents are out of sync with what we say we believe, our kids will spot it faster than anyone, and with uncanny accuracy.

Here are two more ways fathers exasperate their children. One really hits home for most dads because men more than women seem to be prone to the temptation to live out their dreams through their offspring. Pushing a child toward a profession or an area of skill without taking into account how God has designed and equipped that particular child can produce major frustration in both parent and child.

How many fathers dream of their sons achieving glory on the football gridiron or the baseball diamond? Their numbers are legion! We're not talking about just helping a child learn how to swing a bat or throw a ball. Nor is there anything wrong with a father sharing his interests and hobbies with his children. We're talking about pushing, badgering, driving a son or daughter in a direction he or she may not want to go.

The last exasperator we will discuss is time without focus. This is the dad whose actions and body language say, "I'm here, but I really don't want to be." Children have built-in radar on this one too.

The story is told of a busy father who wrote in his journal, "Spent the day fishing with my son. A day wasted." But his son wrote in his journal, "Spent the day fishing with my father. The most wonderful day of my life." The message is obvious: time "wasted" with your children isn't wasted at all.

Train and Admonish Your Children

The second half of Paul's command to parents, and particularly to fathers, in Ephesians 6:4 is where we want to camp for the rest of this chapter. "The discipline and instruction of the Lord" expresses the heart of a father's responsibility and privilege toward his children.

"Discipline and instruction" have to do with training and admonition, which includes correction when the child strays from the right path. It takes courageous parents to discipline, teach, and correct their children today because that flies in the face of almost every example they see in the culture and may even bring them stares of disapproval from other parents.

A friend of ours has a wonderful, godly mother-in-law who is old-school when it comes to discipline. She's not afraid to say to a visiting child who is acting up, "We don't do that in this house."

One time a little girl challenged this woman after being corrected for misbehaving in that woman's home. But she stood her ground and said to the girl, "I'm the adult, you're the child. You will do as I say in my house." Meanwhile, instead of disciplining their daughter for misbehaving and sassing an older adult, the girl's parents glared in anger at my friend's mother-in-law. But that didn't bother her either—and we say, may her tribe increase!

Dear Christian father, your role in the home is not to be your children's buddy, banker, or buffoon. You may say, "But I want to be a hero to my kids." That's great, but let's talk about what makes someone a hero. The usual definition is someone who gets his name in the paper or his face on TV because of his exploits. But using that narrow understanding leaves out most fathers—unless you pull people from a burning building or dive from a helicopter into shark-infested waters to tie a rope around a drowning person.

However, if we define a heroic dad as one who is faithful to his wife, loves the Lord with all his heart, gives his boss his best eight hours every day, and keeps his word and his promises to his children even when it's hard, then any father can qualify as a hero. To be a hero is to know and do the Word of God, to stand on God as your Rock. Dad, your family will stand if you will stand on Jesus Christ.

Joshua was a hero in God's book. Joshua was a warrior and leader, to be sure, but the most heroic thing he ever did was the day he stood before the Israelites at the edge of the Promised Land and challenged the nation to decide whom they would serve: "And if it is evil in your eyes to serve the LORD, choose this day whom you will serve, whether the gods your fathers served in the region beyond the River, or the gods of the Amorites in whose land you dwell. But as for me and my house, we will serve the LORD" (Joshua 24:15).

It takes this same kind of decision and dedication and determination for fathers to build their families on the solid rock of God and His Word today. Here are some basic building blocks any father can use to build a Christ-centered home and be a genuine hero to his children.

Give Your Children Plenty of Love

You might respond, "Everybody knows that!" Maybe so, but not everybody is doing it, especially by God's definition of love. Loving your children is not simply giving them what they want but what they need. A great definition of love is "the willingness to surrender that which has value in life in order to enrich the life of another."

In other words, someone who is loving says to the person loved, "I will give up something of importance to me if that's what it takes to meet your needs." That's really what good parenting is all about. Parents are constantly called on to give it up, to use a modern expression, in terms of their time, energy, and effort. Someone has said that a father is a person who has pictures in his wallet where his money used to be.

In reality, another word for courageous parenting is *sacrifice*. Fathers may be called upon to surrender their personal agendas and even career ambitions when necessary for the good of their families.

An old song talks about what we wouldn't do for love. That is the theme song of a godly father.

Give Your Children Plenty of Affection

A courageous dad isn't afraid to hug his kids. We like the bumper sticker that says, "Kids need hugs, not drugs!"

Fathers need to express love to their children with hugs and kisses. That way, children not only hear Dad telling them he loves them, they feel it!

Some man may say, "That's just not me. I'm not the touchy, hugging kind." Well, get over it! God wants you to take your children in your arms to love and bless them, just as Jesus did with the little children when He laid His hands on them and blessed them with His physical touch as well as with His words (Matthew 19:13-15).

You know the story Jesus told about the prodigal son in Luke 15:11-32. The best part of the story is what this young man's father did when he saw his son coming back home in total disgrace: "But while he was still a long way off, his father saw him and felt compassion, and ran and embraced him and kissed him" (v. 20). The story of the prodigal son is really the story of the faithful father and his extravagant love.

Deb: As a wife and mother as well as a partner with Jack in ministry, I am deeply concerned about the girls in our culture. We've been told that girls who have a healthy relationship with their father, one that includes wholesome expressions of affection, are not likely to go off seeking affection, approval, and intimacy from men in inappropriate ways when they are older. I want to encourage fathers—don't be hesitant to love your daughters! Like Jack, I lost my father when I was a young adult. But what a rich store of memories I have of my dad's love. His love affirmed me and gave me security and helped me see what real love was all about so I could recognize it when I saw it in Jack's life.

Give Your Children Plenty of Encouragement

This is another of the biggies. Children need affirmation and acceptance; they need words of blessing and praise.

Jack: I like to tell dads, you need to be a cheerleader for your kids—without the skirt, please! Your children need to know that you are proud of them and believe in them.

Sometimes we get this encouragement thing twisted up. A good example is the dumbing-down effect we hear so much about in our schools. Somebody somewhere got the idea that we have to turn every child into a "winner" every time, even when that child isn't making the grade. So let's just lower the standard until everyone measures up.

No! Even a child knows when our attempts to put a positive spin on everything are forced. Encouragement sometimes means that we say, "Son, I appreciate your effort. Now let me show you another way to do that."

Maybe a better word than encouragement is *blessing*. In Scripture we read about fathers who passed on a blessing to their sons. Jacob wanted his father Isaac's blessing so much that he cheated his older brother Esau out of it (Genesis 27; see Genesis 49 for another example of a father's blessing).

A good definition of a blessing in the biblical sense is the giving of *favor* to a child, expressing *fondness*, and passing on *faith*. Fathers who bless their children share with them their significance to God and help them see the gifts and abilities with which God has favored them. A blessing is a father's gift of affection and affirmation in the best sense of those terms.

Some father may be reading this and saying, "I never got that kind of blessing from my father." Then you have a marvelous opportunity to break the chains of your past and to begin a wonderful new tradition in your family! Don't let the past dictate your present or your children's future.

A Biblical Plan for the Family

Give Your Children Plenty of Joy

When you build your family on Jesus Christ and your home is filled with His love, joy should be the natural overflow. But sometimes we have to work at joy. We believe a Christ-centered home should be the happiest, most fun-filled place on earth. We tried to make sure we laughed a lot as a family because we wanted our home to be a place where our kids wanted to be and where they wanted to bring their friends. Don't short-change your children when it comes to having joy and laughter in your home. They'll remember the fun a lot longer than the sermons.

Give Your Children a Genuine Faith

Of course, the best gift you can give your children is an authentic faith in Jesus Christ. As parents we are responsible for passing this faith along to the next generation. That means it has to start with us, since you cannot impart what you do not possess.

The great thing about making sure your children know the Lord as their Savior is that you can still be an effective parent a hundred years from now. That's how long your godly influence can be felt as your children, grandchildren, and great-grandchildren pass along the faith they received from you. And actually, a hundred years is nothing because this kind of gift will keep giving for all eternity.

Dad, are you ready for the challenge of being a loving servant and leader to your wife and a godly example to your children? We're going to do everything we can in this book to help you!

3

THE SACRIFICIAL LOVE AND NURTURE OF A WIFE AND MOTHER

JOHN AND CHARLES WESLEY were born into a remarkable family in Lincolnshire, England. Charles was one of the greatest hymn-writers in the history of the church, and John was a great preacher and the founder of Methodism.

John Wesley was born in 1703 as the fifteenth of nineteen children born to Samuel and Susanna. Susanna Wesley was an amazing woman who was herself one of twenty-five children, which is where she may have learned how to organize her own large family. It was said that she gave each child individual attention and also spent several hours per day in private devotions praying for them. However Susanna Wesley did it, it's hard to argue with the results. Under his mother's influence, John quickly developed in spiritual and academic matters. He began learning Greek, Latin, and theology at the tender age of ten, and he graduated from Oxford University at twenty-one.

It's safe to say that Susanna Wesley fit the pattern of the woman described in Proverbs 31:10-31. We could call this woman God's ideal wife and mother, although for many women this passage can be as intimidating as it is inspiring. Most of us would hesitate to use the word *ideal* to describe ourselves, but it's a wonderful goal to reach for. And the good news is that whenever God's Word addresses the roles of men or women in the home, the standards it sets forth are achievable for God's people in the power of the Holy Spirit.

We suspect that any mother reading this book is glad she doesn't have to have nineteen children to prove her excellence in this role! It's worth noting that the Bible doesn't say how many children the "Proverbs 31 woman" had, only that they blessed her (v. 28). Nor does the text say whether all of her activities meant that she had a home-based business or was simply carrying out the affairs of her household. That's the beauty of God's Word. The qualities the Bible gives for a wife and mother who pleases God can be applied in any family in any culture in any day—whether Susanna Wesley's era or ours.

As we complete this section that lays down a biblical pattern and model for parenting, we want to consider the Bible's precepts for a wife and mother, whose influence is so critical to raising children who love and follow the Lord with all their hearts.

One reason it is so important to understand what God says about the proper roles of a man and woman in the home is that the world is saying something radically different, and has been saying it for at least the past thirty years. The result is that the distinctives that set men and women apart are more blurred today than at any time in history.

We thought the unisex movement of the sixties was pretty radical, but some of those ideas seem almost tame compared to the hatchet job that radical feminism and the homosexual agenda have done on the very concept of what it means to be male and female. The foundations of our social structures are shaking, and the tremors are being felt in our Christian homes.

The Bible's straightforward statement that God created mankind as "male and female" (Genesis 1:27) has become the focal point of a moral and spiritual war. And make no mistake about it: any teaching or movement that distorts the distinctiveness of men and women as God created them is ultimately destructive both to men and women, and to society at large.

It's important to say this because in the cultural atmosphere of today, as soon as we open the Bible to address the issues surrounding men and women and their roles, someone starts throwing dust in the air and complains that Bible-believing Christians are trying to set our culture back a hundred years.

Well, that's not true. We're trying to set it back two thousand years—all the way back to Jesus and the New Testament when the definitive Word for husbands, wives, and parents was delivered by inspiration of the Holy Spirit. What the Word of God teaches was revolutionary and countercultural then, and it still is today. And since our focus in this chapter is on women, let's consider the Scripture's teaching on the value, the role, and the incredible influence of a woman in her home.

FOLLOW YOUR HUSBAND'S LEADERSHIP AND WATCH YOUR MARRIAGE GROW

The teaching of the New Testament was revolutionary and countercultural in the days of Jesus and the apostles because in that day women were often treated like possessions that could be discarded at will. But Jesus elevated the position of womanhood in the world, as did Paul and Peter and the other New Testament writers. Jesus always treated women with perfect dignity, and a number of women whose lives had been changed by the Savior supported Him in His ministry (Luke 8:1-3).

Now if you're a Bible student, you probably know that the Bible's primary instruction to wives is "submit to your own husbands, as to the Lord" (Ephesians 5:22). "Wives . . . be submissive to your own husbands" (1 Peter 3:1, NKJV).

There it is, the *s* word. A lot of people are afraid of it, but part of the reason is that the biblical concept of submission has sometimes been so battered and twisted out of shape that it's hardly recognizable. Many pastors will say that whenever they address this subject from the pulpit, they get nailed to the wall.

It's understandable when the president of N.O.W., the National Organization for Women, says as she did a few years ago that the call for submission on the part of women has no place either in the pulpit or

47

the public square today. The problem is that a lot of people in the church really believe the same thing deep down in their hearts.

But the Bible's teaching is clear and inescapable. So our challenge as believers is not to try and improve on God's Word but to understand it as the Holy Spirit gave it, and then to apply the truth to our lives as correctly and fully as we possibly can.

God Calls Us to Submit to One Another

One of the most basic principles of sound Bible study is to pay close attention to the context of the verse or passage being studied. When we apply this principle to both Ephesians 5 and 1 Peter 3, some powerful truths emerge. The first one is that according to Scripture, submission in marriage is mutual. In fact, mutual submission is the standard for all members of the Body of Christ.

We saw in the previous chapter that Paul's instructions to husbands and wives, and to parents and children, flow out of the command in Ephesians 5:18, "Be filled with the Spirit." Paul then began to list some qualities or character traits that are present in the life of a Spirit-filled person. These include joyful singing to the Lord and a heart of gratitude to Him (vv. 19-20).

And then the apostle makes this statement as part of the same sentence: "Submitting to one another out of reverence for Christ" (v. 21). This is addressed to the church, and so the first thing that needs to be said about biblical submission is this: submission is for Christians, not just for wives. We are told to submit to one another, to yield our rights for the benefit of others. Therefore, submission in the home actually begins with a husband who is submitted to the Lordship of Christ and who lovingly leads his wife as Christ does the church.

Deb: A lot of women who read Ephesians 5:21 would stop here and ask, "Doesn't the principle of mutual submission make it wrong for one partner in a marriage to take a superior position over the other partner?"

Like millions of other Christian women, I've had to study and deal with these issues. I've come to see that most of the objections to marital roles as the Bible teaches them are based on a fundamental misunderstanding, which is why I used the word *superior* in the above question.

I've heard Jack teach many times from the pulpit that the Bible's call for a husband to be the head of his home and for a wife to submit to her husband's leadership has nothing to do with the intrinsic value of women as compared to men. Peter called husbands and wives "heirs together of the grace of life" (1 Peter 3:7, NKJV). Both are of equal value in God's eyes, and I'm glad to say that Jack lives this out in our relationship. A husband's leadership is a God-ordained role and responsibility, not a master lording it over his servant. That distortion comes from the world, and unfortunately it is sometimes aided by husbands in the Christian world who abuse their role. But a right understanding helps us as women to lay aside any preconceived ideas we may have and try to understand what God is saying to us.

———

Jack: I want to add a word to both men and women before we go on. It is next to impossible for a woman to respect a man who does not respect her as a woman. Isn't it interesting that although the Bible commands a wife to submit to her husband, there is no command to a husband to rule over, dominate, or control his wife? What the Bible does tell us husbands is to love our wives with self-sacrificing love and tender understanding (Ephesians 5:25; 1 Peter 3:7). So a husband's assignment is to be a lover as well as a leader and to become the kind of man his wife can truly respect.

Submitting to your husband does not mean you become a doormat. But neither does it mean that you become his competitor in the home. Ephesians 5:33 adds a word to wives that is easy to miss at the end of this long passage: "Let the wife see that she respects her husband."

A husband needs a wife who respects him. Respect is one of the deepest needs a man has, and there is no telling what a man can do when his wife is on his team and believes in him. God is so wise in putting us together as husbands and wives, because the wife was created to be the helper, the completer of her husband, not his competer.

I can say from personal experience that a wife who lovingly conducts herself in this manner is an incredible blessing. I thank God for Deb, who through the years has been willing to walk by my side, and sometimes to stand aside, so that I could do what God has called me to do. I can't think of a decision we've made that we've not made together. I value Deb's input and her influence. She has fulfilled a role in life that, in my opinion, is far greater than the one I have tried to fulfill.

Submission Involves a Rank

The word *submit* that is used in Scripture means literally "to set under" or "to rank under." It's a military term, which helps us understand submission in two ways. First, it teaches that God designed a clear ranking in marriage—it is called headship: "The husband is the head of the wife even as Christ is the head of the church" (Ephesians 5:23). Just as there is no way around the fact that an army has those who lead and those who follow, so in a marriage the husband has been designated as the leader.

The second way the military use of this word helps us understand submission and headship in marriage is that rank in the military does not necessarily mean, for instance, that a colonel is a better person than a sergeant. In fact, just the opposite may be the case. But the sergeant is still responsible to submit to a colonel and to follow his leadership because of the colonel's rank, even if the sergeant is a person of greater character or integrity.

In the same way, a wife's calling to submit to her husband is not by any means a statement of her lesser worth. But God has never created anything that He left leaderless or in the hands of a committee where every member has an equal vote. Our late friend Adrian Rogers used to say, "Anything without a head is dead, and anything with two heads is a freak." A marriage has to have direction, and God has ordained the husband to lead his wife and children.

Submission Is Hard for Sinners

This statement needs some explanation . . . or does it?

We're using the term *sinners* here to describe the human condition we all share as fallen, imperfect, essentially self-centered people living in a fallen, imperfect world that feeds our self-centeredness. Put in those terms, what happens when two sinners get married? You bring two imperfect people with strong self-desires together under the same roof, and that can mean trouble.

Apart from the grace of God, it's awfully hard to make a biblically sound marriage work because it requires yielding and understanding on the part of both partners. To say that submitting to someone else is not natural for us is a huge understatement. Ever since Adam and Eve plunged the race into sin, there has been conflict in all human relationships. And that conflict is intensified when one or both people who share the same name and address decide they are going to live for self instead of submitting to God and His plan for their marriage.

One woman said of her marriage, "My husband and I have been one all these years. We just haven't figured out which one!"

Another woman said, "My husband and I have been married for twenty years. There's nothing he wouldn't do for me, and there's nothing that I wouldn't do for him. And that's exactly what we do for each other—nothing!"

If it weren't for marital conflict, stand-up comedians and writers of television sitcoms wouldn't have much material to work with. But there is nothing funny about a home where the husband isn't leading and the wife is battling for control. And the damage of a relationship like that is multiplied if these two are also parents who, for better or worse, are modeling the kind of marriage and family life their children are most likely to catch and reproduce.

So we can say it again—submission isn't easy or natural for any of us. But instead of just saying, "Get over it!" here is some encouraging news: the Holy Spirit can help us get over it. That is, we can grow in our God-given roles as we yield ourselves to the leading and the control of the Holy Spirit. And here is more good news: because marriage is a journey that we make over the years, we have more than enough opportunities to learn how to die to ourselves and become the spouses and parents that God wants us to be.

This means that submission for a wife and loving leadership for a husband are not something we suddenly arrive at one day, so we can say, "I've got it." Instead we have to keep learning and applying, and relearning and reapplying, the truths of God's Word because we are sinners on an incredible journey of grace.

LOVE, NURTURE, AND TEACH YOUR CHILDREN AND WATCH THEM GROW INTO DYNAMIC CHRISTIANS

Since our goal in this opening section is to lay the foundation for courageous parenting, let's talk about two pillars that need to undergird the life of a mother who wants her home and family to be a reflection of the Lord Jesus Christ. These pillars are sacrificial, nurturing love and consistent, patient teaching.

A Mother's Love Is the Heart of the Home

It's almost impossible to talk about a mother's parenting skills without bringing up another s word: sacrifice. Someone has said that *sacrifice* is simply a nine-letter word for mother. Any woman who didn't know going in that motherhood involves sacrifice probably learned that truth very early on.

We've been parents long enough to know that sacrifice, done correctly and biblically, requires love, which is why we added the element of nurturing love to this parental pillar. As important as a sacrificial spirit is for a mother, it's also crucial for those acts of sacrifice to be made in love. Otherwise, making sacrifices for our children can become a grudging duty that actually begins to build resentment on our part toward them.

It may seem that writing about love and sacrifice to a mother is nothing more than "preaching to the choir." In other words, unnecessary.

And we would *almost* agree, for it does seem that if one emotion comes naturally to a human being, it is a mother's love for her child. Enough tender poems and songs have been written about motherly love to bring a roomful of tough guys to tears. And it's true that students in the crowd and players on the sidelines at college football games say, "Hi, Mom" more and hold up more "Hi, Mom!" signs than the next twenty most popular greetings combined.

But we said "almost" for the reason mentioned earlier: we parents are flawed, sinful people with a propensity to seek our own will and way even at real cost to someone else. We need to love as Christ loves, which is why Paul exhorts older women in the church, "Train the young women to love their husbands and children" (Titus 2:4).

So it's important for mothers who want to follow Jesus Christ to realize that the love and nurture they have in their hearts toward their children needs to be cultivated and developed with the help of the Holy Spirit.

Did we mention that motherhood involves sacrifice? This is a principle that God has built into the system. Paul wrote to the Corinthians, who were his spiritual children and were sorely in need of his care, "Now for the third time I am ready to come to you. And I will not be burdensome to you; for I do not seek yours, but you. For the children ought not to lay up for the parents, but the parents for the children" (2 Corinthians 12:14, NKJV).

Laying up what is needed for our children doesn't refer only to our will and the trust funds we execute for the kids after we're gone. For a mother, laying up for her child may mean laying down her plans for the day or laying aside her own wishes in order to meet the child's needs. This is the essence of sacrificial, nurturing love, and many godly moms do it every day of the year without calling attention to themselves or wearing an armband in protest.

You may know the name Howard Hendricks, a popular speaker and author who has been teaching Christian education at Dallas Theological Seminary since 1950. "Prof," as his students affectionately call him, tells of a time early in his ministry when he headed home after a tough day

53

at school, ready to let his wife, Jeanne, know how bad he had it and what an underappreciated servant of the Lord he was.

But when "Prof" Hendricks came in the door that afternoon, he found his wife holding a colicky baby on her lap, gently rocking and rubbing the baby's back while she read her Bible. Dr. Hendricks said he ran to the bedroom, fell on his knees, and cried out to God to make him the kind of person his wife was. A lot of Christian husbands would be wise to offer that same prayer in regard to their wives.

Now don't get the wrong idea. The sacrifice and love a mother shows is not a one-way street or an invitation for those in her household to wipe their feet on her. There is a tremendous honor that is due to a mother, beginning with the command, "Honor your father and your mother, that your days may be long in the land that the LORD your God is giving you" (Exodus 20:12). God gets even more to the point in Exodus 21:15 when He says, "Whoever strikes his father or his mother shall be put to death." As far as we know, no adolescent in ancient Israel put the Mosaic Law to the test on that one.

This is a good time to consider the greatest example of submission and sacrificial, nurturing love the world has ever seen—the willingness of Jesus Christ to leave the glories of heaven, where He was and is coequal with God the Father, to come to earth and take on human flesh. Paul gave us this classic description of Jesus' attitude in becoming our Savior:

> *Have this mind among yourselves, which is yours in Christ Jesus, who, though he was in the form of God, did not count equality with God a thing to be grasped, but made himself nothing, taking the form of a servant, being born in the likeness of men. And being found in human form, he humbled himself by becoming obedient to the point of death, even death on a cross. (Philippians 2:5-8)*

Christ came to die in agony and blood on the cross for the sins of the world—denying His own rights, submitting His perfection and purity to the hands of sinful people. And the best part is that, as the song says, "He did it all for love." This is how much Christ loved the church. And as Christ loved the church, men are to love their wives, wives are to submit to their husbands, and parents are to love and nurture their children.

Teach Your Children Well, and They Will Bless You

The importance of a mother's teaching role with her children cannot be overstated. Despite all the new configurations and definitions of family in our twenty-first-century world, the most common pattern in a home for teaching is still a mother with her children. Part of the reason for that is the continuing epidemic of fatherlessness in our culture. And while this is tragic, it also makes a mother's teaching role all the more crucial.

Twice in the book of Proverbs, Solomon exhorted his son concerning the latter's obligation to hear and obey the teaching of both parents. "Hear, my son, your father's instruction, and forsake not your mother's teaching" (Proverbs 1:8). And then in 6:20, "My son, keep your father's command, and do not forsake the law of your mother" (NKJV).

Clearly, these commands show that the father and mother were both involved in teaching their children, and both of their words carried authority. "The law" of the mother that Solomon referred to was not necessarily the Mosaic Law, but the principles and maxims the mother taught her children that were rooted in the Law of Moses. This is something a godly mother can do today because the principles and truths of God's Word have not changed and are still readily available to us to know and pass on to our children.

We chose the words *consistent* and *patient* to describe a mother's teaching ministry with her children because these terms capture the heart of child training. A child needs consistent instruction—day by day, one building block at a time—because that's the way children learn. But this instruction also needs to be patient, because the fact is that children often knock the building blocks over! Ask a mother who has raised a family how many times she had to put the fork or spoon back in her children's hands after they dropped it or how many spills she cleaned up along the way and you'll get a picture of patience.

Children need consistency and patience, and the best place to find them is in their home under the watchful eye and loving hand of a mother.

The question that many women ask at this point is, are you saying that a mother needs to be at home full-time while her children are growing up?

That's an issue every set of Christian parents has to decide before the Lord. But we believe this is the best situation if at all possible, and we know from experience that God can provide for our needs when we put first things first. Will it be easy? No, but then it really never has been. It takes a very courageous mother to say, "I will lay aside other plans to make my home and children my first priority." If you have a wife like that, you have a special treasure who needs an equally courageous husband to support her.

One classic biblical example of a mother's teaching influence has to be the Lord Jesus and His mother, Mary. The Bible does not give us many details of the Savior's childhood or home life, but there is no doubt that Mary had an enormous impact on Jesus, especially since many Bible scholars believe Joseph may have died at a relatively young age. Mary is often given such exalted religious status that she becomes the last person on earth with whom a mother feels she can identify. But that simply is not the case. Mary was a human mother who along with Joseph, and perhaps alone after his death, taught her children the Law of God.

Another terrific example is the family of Timothy, Paul's spiritual son and fellow worker in the gospel. Paul gave us the quintessential model of a teaching mother when he wrote to Timothy, "I am reminded of your sincere faith, a faith that dwelt first in your grandmother Lois and your mother Eunice and now, I am sure, dwells in you as well" (2 Timothy 1:5). We'll meet Lois and Eunice again, but for now it is enough to note that they instilled the truth of God into Timothy in such a way that it enabled him to stand for the Lord in his ministry at Ephesus.

Sacrificial, nurturing love. Consistent, patient teaching. A mother who exhibits these qualities with her children deserves all the love, support, and encouragement we can give her.

4

THE INCREDIBLE VALUE OF CHILDREN

GEORGE H. W. BUSH has a legacy of service to his country that is unique in American history. He is the only other man besides John Adams, our second President, to be both the President of the United States and the father of a President. And when you add the fact that Mr. Bush was also a two-term Vice President and, as of this writing, the father of a state governor (Jeb Bush of Florida), the elder Mr. Bush is in a category by himself. And this does not include his service as a World War II hero, head of the Central Intelligence Agency, and ambassador to China. With a record like this, the former President was asked in a recent interview, "What is your most important achievement in life?"

George Bush could have reached back over his life and cited any number of great achievements. But in answer to that question, he said, "My children still come home to see me."

That's a pretty profound answer when you think about it. Mr. Bush was totally sincere, which shows that he has his priorities in order. He understands that his most important role in life has not been as a war hero, ambassador, or leader of the free world but as a father.

This is true for every parent, because the day we became fathers and mothers the answer to the question, "What is your most important achievement in life?" changed forever. What will matter most for us at the end of life is not the medals or awards we have received or the portfolio we have built. Our most important and lasting legacy will be our children, which is why the Bible puts so much emphasis on the home and family as opposed to the marketplace.

The priority that God wants parents to place on their home comes through very clearly in Psalm 127, which describes God's blessing on a home and yet begins with this warning: "Unless the LORD builds the house, those who build it labor in vain. Unless the LORD watches over the city, the watchman stays awake in vain. It is in vain that you rise up early and go late to rest, eating the bread of anxious toil; for he gives to his beloved sleep" (vv. 1-2).

Does this message about the futility of labor apart from God sound familiar? It should, because the superscription of this psalm attributes it to Solomon, who also wrote Ecclesiastes with its theme of the vanity of life apart from God's blessing. Verses 1-2 of Psalm 127 are a brilliant executive summary of the message that Solomon communicated in Ecclesiastes.

Just so we're clear, this psalm is not endorsing laziness or the neglect of life's duties. Instead Solomon exhorts us not to try and build either a home life or a work life without seeking God's strength and guidance. The blessing, or reward, for putting our trust in God and depending on Him is a home life of which He is the Builder and Guardian and a work life that is ultimately satisfying without consuming all of our time and energy. Psalm 128 describes this blessing well: "Blessed is everyone who fears the LORD, who walks in his ways! You shall eat the fruit of the labor of your hands; you shall be blessed, and it shall be well with you" (vv. 1-2).

OUR CHILDREN ARE SPECIAL GIFTS OF GOD

With this backdrop of a God-centered and God-dependent life, Solomon saved the best part of his message for last. Psalm 127 continues:

> Behold, children are a heritage from the LORD, the fruit of the womb a reward. Like arrows in the hand of a warrior are the children of one's youth. Blessed is the man who fills his quiver with them! He shall not be put to shame when he speaks with his enemies in the gate. (vv. 3-5)

It's hard to miss the words "heritage," "reward," and "blessed" (or "happy") in these verses that speak of children.

A heritage is an inheritance or a gift, something we did not earn but receive from the hand of a generous giver. Children are gifts from God—not burdens to weigh us down on our way to the top or, even less, the inevitable by-products of marriage. Gifts are to be received with gratitude and cherished, especially when they come from the hand of our God, who is the Giver of "every good gift and every perfect gift" (James 1:17).

The word *reward* reveals another facet of this truth. A reward is a payment, if you will, for doing the right thing. The best illustration of this is Genesis 15:1, when God told Abraham, "I am your shield; your reward shall be very great." The same Hebrew word for "reward" is used here as in Psalm 127:3, which should elevate our view of children to the highest level.

We May Need to Adjust Our Priorities

What happens when we plug God's incredibly high view of children into the reality of the twenty-first-century family? It becomes apparent pretty quickly that many of us need to make some adjustments if we are going to cherish the gifts and enjoy the reward of our children the way the Bible describes.

There were all kinds of social experiments in the sixties and seventies to redefine and reconfigure the traditional "nuclear" family consisting of a father and mother with their children. Many so-called experts said the nuclear family had bombed, and some even predicted that it would sink from its own weight and disappear like other dinosaurs of a past age.

But those experiments failed to produce a new model of the family, which proved a lot more resilient than experts believed. Now we have prestigious institutions like Harvard University reporting on the results of a research study that followed a group of children from ages five or six through their teenage years.

The researchers wanted to know what factors help a child keep moving forward and become successful in life and what factors contribute to juvenile delinquency. The researchers found that children who were doing well in life had fathers who were firm and fair with discipline, mothers who supervised them and were present in their lives, parents who had affection for one another, and families that spent time together.

Your reaction to this might be, "Duh! They could have figured that out by reading the Bible." That's true. It doesn't take a research study to tell us what makes families work. Again, Psalm 127 speaks to this issue. Verses 1-2 give us the picture of people running day and night, depriving themselves even of sleep as they futilely beat their brains out to get ahead and make their mark in the business marketplace.

What an accurate picture of the fast-paced lifestyle that many of us are living today. Many studies verify another truth the Bible has been teaching since the days of Solomon. This is the reality that people's happiness and sense of satisfaction with life does not go up as they accumulate more stuff. It is often the reverse, in fact. Our parents and grandparents had life's basic necessities and few luxuries. Yet they consistently rated their lives as happy and satisfying, while we, their children, are stressed as we try to pay for all the stuff we have. And yet the same surveys show that it takes more things to make us happy.

That's why Solomon said it was vain, or useless, to get up early, stay up late, and spend sleepless nights going after and then trying to support the good life when it's waiting for us right there in our homes.

We Need to Get Fathers Back into the Action

Jack: I'm on a campaign to help husbands and fathers get it together in their families. One father said, "If I had it to do all over again, I would love my wife more in front of my children. I would laugh with my children more at our mistakes and joys. I would listen more, even to the smallest child. I would be more honest about my own weaknesses and stop pretending perfection. I would pray differently for my family: instead of focusing on them, I'd focus on me and my walk with God. I would do more things together with my children. I would do more encouraging and bestow more praise. I would pay more attention to little things, deeds and words of love and kindness. And if I had it to do all over again, I would share God more intimately with my family."

As I read this, my question is, why wait until it's too late to do the right thing when God's Word and the counsel of fathers who have been there tell us to put first things first now? One of the problems in our society today is fathers who are missing in action. When you talk to children and teenagers you hear things like, "My dad doesn't take time for me," "My dad doesn't take me anywhere," or "I can't talk to my dad."

Many fathers would respond, "Well, I may not spend a lot of time with my children, but I give them quality time." But I think quality time is a myth. Children don't know the difference between time and quality time; they just know time!

———

Deb: We are told that the average time a father in America spends with his children is eight minutes per day during the weekdays and fourteen minutes per day on the weekends. I think there are some things we wives can do to help our husbands improve on those figures.

For instance, we can help our husbands identify specific times and activities they can spend with their children in the week or month ahead, and then help Dad keep his schedule clear for those occasions. We also have the opportunity and responsibility to help our husbands evaluate and adjust their priorities as things come up that would take them away from the family. If worse comes to worst and your husband is basically missing in action at home, tell him you're willing to live on less if it means his family can have more of him!

———

This moving poem was written by a father to a nationally syndicated radio host and counselor, Dr. Laura Schlessinger. Whoever this man is, he has gotten the message about the value of children and the few years we have to love and raise them:

A Biblical Plan for the Family

How many more nights do I have, God?
How many more nights do I have to tuck
each of my boys into bed with their teddy bears?

How many more times do I have left, God?
How many more times do I have left to lift my
boys up onto my shoulders before they're too big?

How many more kisses, God?
How many more kisses do I get to give to
my boys after I've tucked them in at night?

How many more pushes, God?
How many more pushes do I get to give
my boys on a swing before they outgrow it?

How many more days, God?
How many more days of hot summer do I have left
to run through the sprinklers with my boys?

How many more tears, God?
How many more tears of joy will I shed at the end
of each day that my boys have grown through?

How many more times, God?
How many more times will I get to lift
my boys back into bed once they've fallen out?

How many more years, God?
How many more years before they come and
lift me from the floor after I've fallen?

How many, God? How many?

This father asked the right Person, because only God knows how many hugs and tears and days we have with our children. But whatever the number of our days may be, they are fleeting because we will not have our children forever. The job of parents is to work themselves out of a job.

Our Children Are on Loan to Us from God

Here is the reason parents need to work themselves out of a job. We never stop being parents as long as we live, but the active role we play in shaping our children's character and getting them ready for their flight from the family nest only lasts for a few short years. (Trust us, young parents. It will seem like a heartbeat when it's over!)

We Are Raising Our Children to Leave, Not to Stay

This final phase of active parenting is pictured very vividly in the last part of Psalm 127: "Like arrows in the hand of a warrior are the children of one's youth. Blessed is the man who fills his quiver with them!" (vv. 4-5a).

Solomon picked his imagery wisely under the Holy Spirit's inspiration. Warriors in the ancient world not only fired arrows in battle, but they made their own. They took great care to make sure that each arrow's shaft was straight so it would fly straight to the target. Arrows weren't fired randomly in battle either, but with a target in mind. This wasn't like target practice, where arrows could be retrieved and fired again. A warrior had only one shot with each arrow, and he couldn't get those arrows back. So he couldn't afford to waste them.

This was true in America during the days of this country's westward expansion. A Bible teacher and counselor who has done a lot of work among the Sioux Indians says that the old Westerns we watched on TV, with hundreds of Indian arrows raining down on the settlers' circled wagons and landing all over the place, was pure Hollywood. A Sioux warrior also had to make each of his arrows, so he only fired one when he had a specific target. As this counselor says, whenever a Sioux warrior fired an arrow, he expected to hear an "Ouch!"

Our children are like arrows in our hands today. Each one must be individually shaped and guided, and how well they fly when they leave us depends a lot on how well we have shaped them to hit the target—that is, to penetrate this culture for the Lord Jesus Christ.

Another interesting feature of arrows in the hand of an ancient warrior is that the arrows could go where the warrior could not go, which was right into the middle of the enemy's ranks. Our children will go places we will never go and do things we will never do. So we need to prepare them for whatever life may bring and wherever they may find themselves when they land in adulthood.

Don't miss the point. Our kids will fly from our hands one day, whether they hit the mark or veer off the trajectory and land off-target. And just like homemade arrows, each child is a unique individual who has to be parented in a unique way. This is another subject in itself, which we will address in the next chapter, so suffice it to say for now that each of our children needs personalized parenting.

We Are the Stewards, Not the Owners of Our Children

This is a tough concept for many parents to accept. But the Bible is clear that our children belong to God, not to us. This is why the act of publicly dedicating children to the Lord when they are born is so important. It's a declaration to the church that we are committed to raise each child in the nurture and instruction of the Lord, which implies that we understand that we will one day give an account to Him of the job we did as parents. And dedicating our children to God is also a witness and reminder to us as parents that parenthood is not a private party we can conduct any way we want but is a trust from the Lord.

The insightful father who wrote the poem quoted above realized that he didn't have an unlimited number of days to raise his children. If you have a swing set or playhouse in the backyard that used to buzz with activity or a basketball goal over the garage that doesn't have a net because it isn't being used anymore, you know what we're talking about.

It's easy to become nostalgic as we think about children who are grown and gone. But that's the goal! They're arrows to be fired in the battle for souls and the soul of this culture. Our job is not to keep our children dependent upon us but to raise them to be dependent upon the Lord Jesus Christ.

OUR CHILDREN ARE TO BE RAISED FOR GOD

American humorist Mark Twain suggested a humorous plan for raising children. He said that when children turn thirteen, they should be put into a barrel. And when they turn sixteen, the hole in the barrel should be plugged!

The truth is that Mark Twain was a loving and doting father to his three daughters, who were born after Twain and his wife lost a son in infancy. Twain's humor has a point, though, because there is more than enough challenge, and sometimes frustration, in raising children who are ready to be sent out into the world as well-shaped and finely sharpened arrows. Most of us parents have had times when we said, "Either put the kids in a barrel, or let me get in there!"

This brings to mind the story of a father who was pacing on a sidewalk one day beside a baby carriage as the baby inside cried at the top of his lungs. The man was walking back and forth, muttering, "It's going to be OK, Albert. Settle down, Albert. Just take it easy, Albert!"

A woman who was witnessing this scene walked up to the father and said, "Sir, I'm so impressed by your patience with little Albert there."

"Oh, no," the frazzled father replied. "*I'm* Albert!"

Teach Your Children to Love God and His Word

We hope your parenting never involves a barrel, although it may require some pacing once in a while! But Moses had a better idea than either Mark Twain or Albert for training children. It was actually God's idea, revealed to Moses in one of the greatest passages in all of Scripture:

> *And these words that I command you today shall be on your heart. You shall teach them diligently to your children, and shall talk of them when you sit in your house, and when you walk by the way, and when you lie down, and when you rise. You shall bind them as a sign on your hand, and they shall be as frontlets between your eyes. You shall*

write them on the doorposts of your house and on your gates.
(Deuteronomy 6:6-9)

This is the God-ordained method for giving our children consistent direction and spiritual training. The content of that training is stated in the previous verses: "Hear, O Israel: The LORD our God, the LORD is one. You shall love the LORD your God with all your heart and with all your soul and with all your might" (vv. 4-5).

This is the heart of the matter when it comes to the spiritual training that we are called to give our children. If you are successful in raising children who love the Lord their God with every fiber of their being, you have done an award-winning job as a parent.

But notice that there is nothing magical or mystical about the way we need to teach our children. What the Bible is saying is that children need both a model and a mentor. They need a model to give them an example to look up to and a goal to strive for, and they need a mentor to train them in reaching that goal.

The home is the best place on earth for this kind of teaching, because it is the place where we lie down and get up—in other words, where the daily routines of life are lived out. And parents are the God-appointed teachers of this spiritual life curriculum. The church's role is to come alongside the family to help teach the teachers and mentor the mentors. There is nothing more exciting on earth than when a home and a church are working together to produce godly children.

We've often heard the old saying that the really important lessons of life are caught rather than taught. It's fine to say this, and we know that children usually imitate our example more than they listen to our words. But that doesn't mean we can neglect the teaching.

Deb: The need to teach our children at every stage of life was really driven home to me after the fearful attacks of 9/11. Through the years before that terrifying day, I relaxed as a parent. I think I went on autopilot. I was still trying, reading, and listening, but somehow I forgot the impact that my children and my friends' children would have on the world in which we live. *Someday* was a piece of time in the distance; surely it was not here and now.

Then 9/11 happened, and every alarm in my soul went off. Along with every other American, I ached from the core of my being. I was in shock and fearful, but most of all I was troubled in a way I had never experienced before. Being raised and educated, and now living, in a society where peace was the core of our existence, my very base was shaken. As a parent my thoughts and actions turned at once to my children.

Even though I was hundreds of miles away from the sites of the 9/11 attacks, I yearned to gather my chicks close to home. For as far as I was concerned, my family was under attack. There was no plane flying into my house, but there was an enemy at the door.

The Scriptures clearly tell us that in the end times there will be rumors of wars, and violence will escalate. Surely what I saw before me on every news outlet was an example of what hate could do to mankind. On the evening of that eventful day, I took a long stroll with my dog and pondered my response. After hours of contemplating, I was led to sit down at my computer and compose a letter the likes of which I had never written to my children.

Years later I wonder if they thought their mother was losing her stability when they received that sentimental, often extremely serious piece from my heart. In this most private piece of correspondence, I poured my heart out to them. I challenged them to live their lives as if the world depended upon them. Not the world of riches and glamour, but the world their dad and I had endeavored to lead them through. I told them it had to be a life of dependence upon God to meet their every need—a life of love, commitment, and honesty.

It took 9/11 to awaken me to the seriousness and brevity of life, and how as a parent I must never be off my guard. It is my children and their generation who will face the full onslaught of lies, hate, and evil that man is capable of spewing out. It will be the legacy of parents today that enables the work of God to move forward in the ages to come. May we be found faithful!

Jack: It is amazing to me as a pastor how many Christian families don't take time to read and study God's Word together. I know that many fathers in particular feel inadequate and intimidated at the thought of leading their families in worship and devotions, and so they never make an attempt.

But my fellow father, let me tell you that you can do it! You don't have to stand and preach to lead your family in time around the Word of God and in prayer. If you're nervous, ask your wife and even the children to help you.

There are so many good Bible storybooks and other teaching helps available at your local bookstore that you couldn't carry them all out the door. Ask your pastor or children's minister for guidance. But the important thing is to start. Let your kids see that you love and value God's Word, and they'll remember that for the rest of their lives.

Someone has said that if you want people to bleed, you need to hemorrhage. If you want your children to love God and His Word, you need to glow with white-hot fire for Him. That's why the order of Deuteronomy 6 is so important. Notice that the command to love God is made to us as parents *first*, before we are told to teach it to our children. When our passion for Jesus Christ is aflame in our hearts, that provides an attitude and atmosphere in the home that makes it conducive for a child to fall in love with Christ and go out on fire for Him.

Anne Graham Lotz, the daughter of Billy and Ruth Graham and a wonderful Bible teacher and speaker in her own right, was once asked how she developed her deep love for God's Word. We might think she would have mentioned her father's sermons, but she didn't. Mrs. Lotz said she developed her love for God's Word when as a little girl she would walk by her mother's room and see her with her Bible open and all the commentaries of Scripture around her as she pored over the Scriptures day after day. Then Mrs. Lotz added, "Because of my mother's devotion and dedication to the Word of God, it implanted in me a desire to know and to love God's Word as well."

That's the right kind of example, because it went past lectures and sermonizing and penetrated right to the heart of a little girl. That's the idea behind Deuteronomy 6. The word "teach" in verse 7 means "to sharpen." It speaks of a penetrating cut, something that goes right down to the deepest part of a person's being. Make sure that your teaching about God and His Word comes from a life that has itself been deeply cut and penetrated by Him, and your children will follow your example.

Our Children Need Firm and Loving Discipline

One of the inescapable realities of life is that if you don't discipline your children, somebody else will discipline them for you.

The Bible teaches the importance of firm and consistent discipline. Now we might as well acknowledge right up front that the issue of whether to spank children will never be settled to everyone's satisfaction. Generally speaking, in the world's mind-set spanking is never permissible, period. On the other extreme are misguided parents who go far beyond a few well-placed applications of the board of education to the seat of knowledge and abuse their children in the name of discipline.

Those are the extremes, but here is the Word of God on the subject: "Folly is bound up in the heart of a child, but the rod of discipline drives it far from him" (Proverbs 22:15). It is natural for children to make foolish decisions and foolish choices, and therefore they need discipline. Spanking certainly isn't the only tool of discipline parents have, and we believe that spankings should be few and far between. But when they happen, they ought to be a big deal in terms of reinforcing the right attitude and behavior and disciplining the wrong.

Deb: Our experience as parents has been that if you begin early with spanking or any form of discipline, it saves you a lot of heartache and anxiety later on. Jack was usually the disciplinarian in our house when it came time for a spanking, and he always did it in a firm and loving way that I believe had a very powerful and positive effect on our two sons in particular.

We see a lot of young parents today giving their children time-outs when they have misbehaved. I doubt if any formal studies have been done on the effectiveness of time-outs, but I fear that too often it is used to help a parent avoid the painful but important task of applying discipline in a way the child will remember and learn from.

Many young parents are afraid of making their children angry at them or fear that their children won't like them if they apply discipline. I encourage you not to let that keep you from disciplining your children. They'll get over the hurt and learn the lesson, and they'll love you for it later.

Every child needs to be raised with two pats on the back—one low enough to correct the wrong and one high enough to praise the right.

Another word of wisdom from the book of Proverbs also contains what some people may consider to be controversial advice: "Do not withhold correction from a child, for if you beat him with a rod, he will not die. You shall beat him with a rod, and deliver his soul from hell" (23:13-14, NKJV).

We need to say it again: this passage does not give parents permission to abuse their children. The emphasis here is not on the size of the rod or the number of strokes but on the importance of not neglecting your child's discipline.

If the writer had said, "Do not withhold food from a child," everyone would say "Amen" because we all know a child needs food to live and thrive. No loving parents would withhold food or any other essential thing their child needs. Well, the same is true for discipline. The fact is that if you love your child, you will discipline your child.

One more important verse on discipline from Proverbs says this: "The rod and reproof give wisdom, but a child left to himself brings shame to his mother" (29:15).

"A child left to himself." What a perfect description of the phenomenon we have been seeing in this country for some time now—children and teenagers left to themselves. They go home alone, let themselves in, and learn their morals from MTV. They used to be raised at their mother's knee. Now they're raised at some other joint!

Children left to themselves bring sorrow to themselves and their parents, but a disciplined child is a delight. We would agree that God is the ultimate loving Parent. Does He discipline His children? The writer of Hebrews answers, "My son, do not regard lightly the discipline of the Lord, nor be weary when reproved by him. For the Lord disciplines the one he loves, and chastises every son whom he receives" (Hebrews 12:5-6).

The Lord's discipline is not meant to make us hard and resentful but to soften our hearts so that we become tender toward Him. This is what we want to accomplish in the hearts of our children by our firm, consistent, and loving discipline. Children are far too valuable to be abused, neglected, or left on their own to try and figure out what life is all about.

So we plead with you as a parent, ask God to change your heart, rearrange your schedule, alter your lifestyle, and make whatever other sacrifices may be necessary to give your children the priority in your time, attention, and affections that they need and deserve. Then when they are launched and you look back, you will be able to say, "I have no greater joy than to hear that my children are walking in the truth" (3 John 4).

PART TWO

PUTTING THE PLAN
TO WORK

5

PARENTING:
AN UNCOMMON CALLING

SEVERAL YEARS AGO as a series of wildfires was sweeping through southern California, a story appeared on television about a particular neighborhood in which one home was left standing, virtually untouched by the fire, while about twenty homes around it burned to the ground. This home had a little discoloration due to smoke damage and a singe here and there, but it stood alone in the middle of this neighborhood with burned-out houses all around it.

The television crew wanted to find out why this house had stood against the fire. So they interviewed the owner and discovered that when he built the house, he had taken extra precautions to ensure that it was protected not only against earthquakes but against fire. These extra steps included double-paned windows, thick stucco walls, special eaves, a concrete tile roof, and abundant insulation.

This house was so extraordinary that when the firefighters battling the blaze realized it was standing against the fire, they actually rallied to it and used this man's home as the place from which to fight the flames that were sweeping through the neighborhood as they were driven by strong winds.

That's a great picture of the kind of homes we want to build as Christian parents—homes that can stand firm as the fires of hell and the winds of culture are unleashed against them. Satan wants to hammer our kids, and while we can't stop the fire from spreading, we can stop it at our doorsteps. By God's grace and power we can keep the fires from burning our houses down. But in order to do that, we need courageous parents.

Our families are in a spiritual fire zone today. So we need to pay close attention to how we build our homes. The Bible gives us the right building plan for any structure: "According to the grace of God given to me, like a skilled master builder I laid a foundation, and someone else is building upon it. Let each one take care how he builds upon it. For no one can lay a foundation other than that which is laid, which is Jesus Christ" (1 Corinthians 3:10-11).

Dads and moms, you are called to be the wise builders of your home. So we want to give you some tools to help you construct a biblically-based home and family, no matter where you are in the parenting process.

Previous generations learned, "The hand that rocks the cradle rules the world." Well, the cradle has been rocked pretty hard over the past forty years, and it hasn't always been by a mother's gentle hand. Once our culture bought into the idea that motherhood was not a fulfilling role for a woman, we witnessed one of the most jarring social changes in history as millions of women—many of them mothers—left home and entered the workforce. The cradle became a car seat, and when the kids got older they went to school with house keys hanging around their necks. The glass in the family portrait was shattered, so to speak, and we have been picking up the broken pieces for a long time now.

But there are signs that the pendulum is beginning to swing back the other way. A March 2004 cover story in *Time* magazine reported on what appears to be a growing trend: women who, faced with the choice of continuing their careers or staying home to care for their children, are choosing their children. The cover photo on that issue really brought the issue into focus, showing a little child holding on to his mom's business skirt for dear life.

No one ever said being a parent is an easy assignment or that it doesn't require hard choices and commitment. But these things are exactly what make parenting such a great and fulfilling challenge—truly an "uncommon" calling and the best job in the world.

WE CAN LEARN FROM GOOD PARENTS IN THE BIBLE

God's Word gives us fascinating glimpses into the lives of parents and parents-to-be at every stage of family life who applied godly principles in their homes and saw God bless them and their children for it. The ancient Israelites grasped the importance of prayer and care for their children before they were even born. They understood in a profound way not only that a child's life begins at conception but that God's work in that child's life begins in the womb.

Your Children Can Be a Blessing in the Womb

The ultimate examples of expectant parents who were sensitive to God's work are Joseph and Mary, the stepfather and mother of Jesus, and Mary's relative Elizabeth and her priest husband, Zechariah. One of the most amazing parts of the Christmas story is Mary's visit to Elizabeth, when John the Baptist leaped for joy in Elizabeth's womb when she heard Mary's greeting and Elizabeth was filled with the Holy Spirit and pronounced a blessing on Mary (Luke 1:39-45).

Joseph was a person of faith who believed God's word to him and experienced supernatural divine direction (Matthew 1:18-25). His obedience played a major role in the circumstances leading up to the Savior's birth. And even though Zechariah stumbled at the angel Gabriel's promise of a son (Luke 1:5-20), he was also filled with the Spirit and delivered a powerful prophecy of God's work through John the Baptist, the son given to Elizabeth and Zechariah in their old age.

Recognize the Great Value of Children's Earliest Years

The father and mother of Moses are wonderful examples of godly parents with a child in the earliest years and even months of childrearing.

You probably recall the incredible story of baby Moses' protection by his parents and how God rewarded their faith by allowing his mother to nurse him (Exodus 2:1-10).

We can only imagine what Moses' mother taught him in those early years. It must have stuck because when it came time for Moses to take a stand as an adult, he chose to identify with the people of God rather than yielding to the pleasures of Egypt. According to Hebrews 11:24-26, Moses made his decision by faith—his faith in the God of Israel that was instilled in him by his mother. There was no other way he could have learned it.

Hannah is another godly model of a parent with a very young child. She was unable to conceive and prayed fervently for a child (1 Samuel 1:1-18). When God gave her Samuel, Hannah kept her vow to give him back to the Lord to serve Him (vv. 19-28). She saw to it that Samuel was set apart for the Lord from the day he was born. Although Hannah's outward circumstances were very different from today, she shows us the importance of dedicating our children to the Lord. There is no doubt that she taught Samuel what it meant to know God when he was a toddler because he was able to serve in the tabernacle even as a child (v. 28).

Make the Most of Your Children's School-Age Years

Jesus' father and mother come back into the picture when we think of Bible parents with children in the pre-adolescent and adolescent years. The incident recorded in Luke 2:39-52 occurred when Jesus was twelve years old and indicates that He knew the Word of God. Many stories, songs, and other pieces of literature have been written about what life must have been like for the boy Jesus in His home and in Joseph's carpentry shop. The one thing we know for certain is that Mary and Joseph raised Jesus in the fear and instruction of the Lord.

Continue to Teach and Nurture Your Older Children

Another parent in Scripture who modeled biblical childrearing was Eunice, the mother of Paul's ministry companion and spiritual son,

Timothy. She is a great example for any parent to follow, but we want to look at her particularly as the parent of an older child, perhaps even a young adult. When Paul arrived in Timothy's hometown of Lystra, the latter was living at home and was certainly still under his mother's spiritual influence. Timothy was old enough to go with Paul and begin his ministry at this point, so he was definitely an older child.

Eunice is somewhat obscure in the biblical text, being identified only as "a Jewish woman" when Timothy was first introduced (Acts 16:1). Even though Eunice was not named there, the Bible says she was a believer, the most important thing that can be said about any parent.

More is revealed about Eunice in the book of 2 Timothy, where Paul gratefully acknowledged Timothy's strong spiritual heritage (1:5). But the real insight into Eunice's parenting comes later in that epistle when Paul warned about those who were not true to the faith and wrote to Timothy, "But as for you, continue in what you have learned and have firmly believed, knowing from whom you learned it and how from childhood you have been acquainted with the sacred writings, which are able to make you wise for salvation through faith in Christ Jesus" (2 Timothy 3:14-15).

What a statement! If the home is the university of life, then Eunice had a Ph.D. in parenting. She heard the uncommon call and responded to it by doing an incredible job of training Timothy. And please notice that Timothy's grandmother, Lois, also came in for the same well-deserved praise. Lois had done the same great job of training Eunice in the faith (1:5), and Eunice passed it on. Timothy became a dynamic leader of the church with a powerful influence. And it all started in his home as his mother opened the Scriptures and implanted them in Timothy's mind and heart.

Would you like to know Eunice's secret for producing a Timothy? You probably have it on your desk or table, conveniently bound between two covers—your Bible. This means that you as a parent have the same opportunity to do for your children what Eunice did for Timothy. The key is that Timothy's mother taught him "the Holy Scriptures" (3:15, NKJV), which would have been the Old Testament since the New

Testament had not yet been fully recorded. As a Jewish believer who obviously knew God's Word well, Eunice would have known the instruction that Moses gave to the Israelites to teach their children in a systematic, consistent way (Deuteronomy 6:6-9). The key to Eunice's success with Timothy was the regular and faithful teaching she did as part of the family's daily routine as Timothy was growing up.

Jack: There is a lesson in Timothy's story that I hope will be an encouragement to single moms and to wives whose husbands are not fulfilling their role as spiritual leaders in the home. The Bible says in Acts 16:1 that Timothy was "the son of a Jewish woman who was a believer, *but his father was a Greek*" (emphasis added).

This last phrase is set in contrast to Eunice's faith. It could mean that Timothy's father was an unbeliever or not around or both. Judging by his absence in Paul's commendation of Timothy's spiritual heritage, it is clear that Timothy's father had little or no part in his son's biblical training. Being a Greek (or Gentile) meant that this man did not grow up immersed in the Hebrew Scriptures.

But despite the spiritual absence of Timothy's father, look what his mother accomplished by her godly example and teaching. Single mother, be a Eunice! God will honor your commitment to teach His Word to your children. And if you are blessed to have a Christian mother, as Eunice had in Lois, or a godly mother-in-law, let her help you instill God's Word in your children.

Even though your time is no doubt limited as you try to be mom and dad to your kids, the biblical model of incorporating Scripture and its principles into your family's daily routine allows you to multiply the impact of the moments you have.

If you are a Christian wife married to an unbelieving or spiritually insensitive husband, my encouragement is the same. Be a Eunice! You will not only bless your children, but the Bible says that your godly influence is the most powerful witness you can have to your husband (1 Peter 3:1-2).

Along with incorporating Scripture into the family's daily routine, here's another key to the success Eunice had in equipping Timothy for life and service to the Lord. She no doubt drew on principles for child-rearing revealed in the book of Proverbs, which was written from parents to children to instruct them in the way of the Lord.

THE PROVERBS ARE FILLED WITH PRINCIPLES FOR WISE PARENTING

These same principles are available to us today because we too can turn to Proverbs and learn from the same text that godly parents like Eunice studied. Let's draw out principles from Proverbs that help make for successful parenting.

Treat Each Child as a Unique Individual

One of the timeless parenting principles found in Proverbs is also one of the most frequently quoted verses in the Bible: "Train up a child in the way he should go; even when he is old he will not depart from it" (Proverbs 22:6).

Deb: This verse is sometimes taken to mean that if parents make sure their children are in Sunday school and church every week while they're growing up, they will come back to the Lord someday even if they go off the track when they are older.

Jack and I would be the first people to vouch for the importance of regular church attendance! But the church's ministry must be paired with consistent teaching and modeling at home. It's not a matter of either/or but both/and when it comes to the importance of the church and home working in partnership to raise children who are fully devoted followers of Jesus Christ.

Proverbs 22:6 is talking about a child's "way," what we call his or her bent. This is the way God has made a child, with a unique personality, temperament, and other traits. We need to know our child's bent so we can tailor our instruction to be most effective with each child.

As a mother of three I discovered very quickly what every parent knows—our children are all very different. A family that has more than one child usually has one who is compliant and one who is more defiant and strong-willed.

Because of this, the same parenting methods and styles don't work for every child. As parents we want to learn what motivates and interests our children so we can coach and guide them in cooperation with the way God made them instead of trying to make them all alike or just like us.

Proverbs 22:6 could be paraphrased, "Know your children! Study each child so well that you come to know how God made him or her, how He fashioned him or her. Teach your children God's truth in the way your children learn best, and it will stay with them for life." With this in mind, here are five more key parenting principles.

Teach Your Children What It Means to Fear God

The introduction to the book of Proverbs states the reason these words of godly wisdom were recorded: "To know wisdom and instruction, to understand words of insight, to receive instruction in wise dealing" (1:2-3). This is the starting point, the priority, for anything we attempt to do for God. And lest there be any uncertainty about the source of this instruction, Solomon went on to write, "The fear of the LORD is the beginning of knowledge" (v. 7).

Most parents would agree there is nothing quite like having children to put the fear of the Lord in you! But that's all right because we as parents need to fear God in the sense of having a deep reverence and respect for Him and a sense of awe in His presence, which is what the Bible means by fearing God. All education begins here as we teach our children to know and fear God. It is in the reverence and awe of God that lives are changed.

The knowledge and fear of God are so closely connected because we must know Him properly to fear Him adequately. It may seem like a long way from the fear of God to driver's education—unless you've been through it with a teenager or three! One of the first lessons we try to drill into the head of a teenager who wants to drive is to understand and respect—that is, to fear—the awesome power of the machine he or she is so eager to handle.

Our late and dear friend Dr. Adrian Rogers used to say that if a dad is trying to explain to his teenage son how the brake on a car works, and the boy says, "Aw, Dad, I don't want to know about the brake—I want to know about the gas pedal," that boy is not ready to drive!

A driver who doesn't have a healthy respect for the power of a car can wreak incredible damage. The same is true of a failure to fear and reverence God. There's hardly a problem we face today in our culture that isn't somehow connected back to a loss of reverence and fear of Almighty God.

For example, both the violence occurring today in the womb through abortion and the violence on our streets stem from a loss of reverence for God as the Creator of life and therefore a loss of reverence for the sanctity of human life.

Problems such as the abuse of drugs and various addictions and sexual perversions of all kinds signal a loss of respect for the personhood and the body God has given us, which the Bible says is to be a temple of the Holy Spirit that God paid a great price to redeem through Christ's death (1 Corinthians 6:19-20).

If you don't teach your children anything else, teach them the fear of God. Reverence God in your home, and make sure your children see a living example of what it means to honor God in words and actions.

One way you can do this is to be careful in your language. This is a big one because the first words out of most people's mouths today to express surprise or shock or even joy is "O God!" God's name is holy and to be revered, which is why the Third Commandment says, "You shall not take the name of the LORD your God in vain" (Exodus 20:7).

We also revere God when we set aside time to worship Him and honor Him with the first portion of our time, talents, and treasures. Every time our children see us devaluing God or moving Him to the margins of our lives, it lowers their understanding of who God is. Make sure your home is permeated with the fear of God, and neither you nor your children will have to fear anyone or anything else.

Help Your Children Live Lives of Moral Purity

The second chapter of Proverbs is a warning from a father to his son about sexual immorality and its devastating consequences. For the sake of your children's well-being, teach them moral purity. When all is said and done, the best filter for the Internet and the television is still a set of caring parents who are involved and engaged with their children and know what is going into their minds and hearts on a regular basis.

We have a friend with two young adult children who did not allow them to watch a very popular television program when they were growing up. He sampled a few of the episodes to see what the program was like since so many people were watching it, and he was thoroughly disgusted by the dialogue, profanity, and irreverence of the characters.

At the same time, this friend was a leader in his church's youth ministry, and he says he was heartsick one evening as he drove a group of church teens from place to place on visitation ministry. Two eighth-grade boys in the back of the church van spent the entire time discussing their favorite episodes of this same program, and they repeated incredible amounts of dialogue from the show for so long that it got on everyone else's nerves. And as our friend said, these two boys were from "pillar of the church" families.

It's possible that these boys' parents would have disagreed with our friend about the offensive nature of this program. Or maybe they didn't even know their sons were watching it. There will always be disagreements about the entertainment offered by pop culture, but when we apply the biblical principle of occupying ourselves with "whatever is true, whatever is honorable, whatever is just, whatever is pure, whatever is lovely, whatever is commendable" (Philippians 4:8), this will eliminate a lot of stuff that may not seem all that terrible in itself. It's just not worth wasting our time on.

Now the cruel fact is that many parents don't train their children in purity because the parents have compromised in their own lives. Too many Christian parents have buckled under the pressure of the culture until they feel like they have nothing left to fight with in the battle for their children.

But we can't give up because this is a winnable battle! Fight for your children's moral purity, and set the example in speech, dress, and conduct. Paul wrote to Timothy as a young pastor, "set the believers an example in speech, in conduct, in love, in faith, in purity" (1 Timothy 4:12). Dad, you are the pastor and the leader in your home. Your example of purity will set the pace for everyone else.

Teach and Model Integrity in Your Home

The book of Proverbs also speaks plainly to the issue of integrity. "Put away from you crooked speech, and put devious talk far from you" (4:24).

We live in a spin zone in America. Everyone has a spin to put on their story to justify their actions. But if you spin around long enough, you get confused and lose your balance, which is what we see happening in our culture. And our children are spinning around with us.

Integrity refers to wholeness, with no missing parts. Kids need to hear it over and over again: "It's always right to do what's right. It's never right to do what's wrong." A person whose integrity is intact doesn't have to worry about getting his story wrong and getting into trouble. "Whoever walks in integrity walks securely, but he who makes his ways crooked will be found out" (Proverbs 10:9).

This is another area where we need to check ourselves regularly as parents. Lots of people who would never cheat in business or on their taxes may be guilty of exaggerating the truth on occasion, passing on unfounded gossip about another person, or trying to put up a front. Children can spot hypocrisy in a heartbeat, and they are good imitators of what they see and hear. Run a regular integrity check on your life, and make sure your kids are seeing a consistent example—not a perfect example, but one marked by integrity.

Teach Your Children the Value of Being Responsible People

Proverbs 6:6-11 ought to be required reading at every family's dinner table. These verses describe the blessing and reward of hard work, and the ruin that comes from laziness.

We all know what a work ethic is. It's something our grandparents taught our parents! But for the sake of your children's future chances at happiness and success on any level, instill in them a strong work ethic. Help them learn to accept responsibility for their schoolwork, their rooms, and the chores that are part of family life. Then hold them accountable for fulfilling the responsibilities you have given them.

One of the rudest shocks some kids will ever have is when they get out into the workforce and discover that their boss won't come to their house to get them up and dressed when they're running late or just ground them for a week when they mess up. Don't let your children's first taste of responsibility and consequences come when they go off to college or that first job!

Make It a Point to Instill Generosity in Your Children

A major part of the curriculum in the university of life, your home, is to teach your children financial management and generosity. Proverbs 3:9 tells us, "Honor the LORD with your wealth and with the firstfruits of all your produce."

Children need to learn how to give, save, and spend money. For some, saving seems to come naturally. Spending seems to be a universal trait. Teaching children to be generous toward the Lord in their tithing and giving and generous toward others in need is the part of this curriculum that parents will probably have to focus on the most.

Jack: I'm so glad that my parents taught me to take the first 10 percent of my allowance, which was a nickel, and put it in the offering plate at church as my tithe to the Lord. That lesson has stayed with me all through the years. The offering time at your church is a great teaching moment for your children. If they see you giving with joy and faithfulness to the Lord, they will want to follow your example.

———

Deb: Jack and I were married after my freshman year of college at Hardin-Simmons University in Abilene, Texas. He was a much older man, having just completed his sophomore year! The truth is, we were babes. In fact, I can't imagine any of our children being married at that age. But back in the old days when we were teenagers, it was not that uncommon.

With our youth and zeal, though, life was good. It was during those early years that we molded our lives together. We had wonderful times on top of the world and in deep valleys, which forced us to grow up years beyond our ages.

One of the valuable qualities of youth is that we were still teachable. On one particular occasion we got it into our heads that we needed to upgrade our housing. But being full-time college students did not afford us a hefty income. In fact, we only had the roof over our heads because Jack was on a baseball scholarship at Hardin-Simmons, and we could reside in student housing for a mere fifty dollars a month. And that enormous amount could be placed on our student accounts.

Student housing meant a two-bedroom, renovated, army-barracks house on a dirt street in a West Texas town. All the little houses in a row reminded you of an old black-and-white movie when they panned to "the poor side of town." Little did we know that many of our neighbors would go on to become entertainers, professional basketball players, and professors. They were just fellow newlyweds struggling to make ends meet.

By the end of our second year in this housing addition we had the grand idea that we needed to move uptown, into a duplex in a nicer neighborhood. The only thing was, it also meant paying more than fifty dollars a month in rent. We searched until we found the right duplex. It had a real shower (instead of the aluminum one we had in the barracks), a cute little yard with a flowerbed, and real air-conditioning (instead of a window unit that shocked you every time you watered it down with the garden hose). We were "movin' on up!"

The weekend we were going to sign the lease, my father decided he would come and have a look. We excitedly showed him every fine point of the duplex, emphasizing how much safer it would be for me when Jack was out of town playing baseball. After touring the spacious duplex (thinking back, it might have been 1,000 or fewer square feet), he asked us to sit down and draw up a budget.

We listed all our monthly expenditures. There were the normal utilities, Friday night date money, and fees for school. Then being the mathematician he was, Dad laid it all out neatly on the back of a napkin and drew a big circle around the amount we needed. Then he asked us how much we received from the weekend pastorate where Jack served.

Comparing the two amounts, Dad scratched his head and said, "Well, it looks like you can just make it." Then he went on to say, "However, we forgot one important item, and I know you won't want to omit this. It's your tithe." Needless to say, we didn't get the duplex.

Years later when our children were older we took a trip out to our college and drove them around the campus. Enthusiastically we took them over to student housing, where to our amazement the little barrack houses still stood. They had a fresh coat of paint, and the street was now paved. We located the one in which we spent our college years and drove up to the front. It was apparent by the curtains in the windows and the flowers in the yard that some young college couple still called it home.

I turned to the backseat to ask the kids what they thought about our first home. Josh was speechless, and Kelly replied with a look of anguish, "Weren't you just miserable?"

I looked at Jack and smiled, and the picture of my father sitting at the table in that tiny kitchen, writing on the back of a napkin, raced across my mind. That day a lesson about giving was imparted that continues to guide us to this day.

Of course, being generous goes beyond our money. Help your children learn to be generous with their love and service to friends, family, and strangers, which can be done appropriately with your oversight and guidance. Selfishness is a built-in human trait, so we need to implant generosity beside it.

Do you want to answer the uncommon calling of parenting with a powerful influence and example? Teach your children the principles of reverence, purity, integrity, responsibility, and generosity, and you will produce young adults who are ready to stand and shine for the Lord no matter where He takes them.

6

TAKING A STAND IN YOUR HOME

TEXANS ARE PRETTY TOUGH people who have been through a lot, including the hardy souls who survived the great Dust Bowl that devastated large sections of the Midwest, Oklahoma, and Texas in the 1930s.

The term *Dust Bowl* was first used by an Associated Press reporter to describe the impact of the immense dust storm that struck the Texas Panhandle on April 14, 1935. The swirling wall of dust was over a mile and a half high and was driven by sixty-mile-per-hour winds. It completely blotted out the sun and terrified the families who saw it coming. Children literally suffocated in dust drifts just yards from their front door. That terrible day was called "Black Sunday," and those who lived through it never forgot the day when it seemed the world was coming to an end.

The Dust Bowl was a nightmare for farmers on the southern plains, lasting throughout the 1930s. Black Sunday was one of the worst of those times, although other giant dust storms also carried off millions of tons of topsoil, enveloped communities in thick darkness, and devastated lives. One storm blew dust all the way to Chicago, where enough dirt fell on the city to average four pounds per resident.

The great Dust Bowl of the Depression era holds an important lesson as we think about the family today. This agricultural disaster did not arise overnight with no explanation or cause. The dust storm that struck Texas on Black Sunday was just one result of a long, steady process of destructive farming methods and extended drought that turned once-fertile plains into barren wastelands. The plains had been stripped of their natural vegetation for farming, then plowed and planted for so long that when the rains stopped and nothing grew, the soil was left dry and loose and thus was easily carried away by the prairie winds. It wasn't until soil conservation methods were introduced that the region began to recover once the long drought was broken.

We are seeing a lot of dust-bowl type of devastation among families today—a huge cloud of confusion driven by the strong winds of a culture that has been all but stripped of essential spiritual nutrients. The process has been going on for some time now, and the family breakdown we are witnessing today is the result of decades of destructive cultural trends and family choices that may have seemed small at the time but actually began an erosion process that has reached huge proportions.

That's why teenage suicides are at an all-time high. That's why so many children and young people are stumbling and falling today, like Dust Bowl victims being enveloped in a dark cloud. This generation of youth is truly a "lost generation," and the question is, who is going to stop it, and when and how is it going to stop?

It's going to stop when we take a stand in our homes and say like Joshua, "As for me and my house, we will serve the LORD" (Joshua 24:15). That's what it will take to raise a generation of men and women who are called of God and will draw the same line at the front door of their homes.

This is the good news. The dark cloud of family breakdown doesn't have to engulf our homes. And because families stand or fall one at a time, when we commit ourselves to raise children who love and serve God in their generation and will pass the faith along to their children, we can help stop the erosion that has depleted our world of the knowledge and fear of God.

The words of Joshua 24:15 have probably been knitted, crocheted, needle-pointed, carved in wood, framed in photos or paintings, and cast in plaster as much as or more than any other words in the Bible. This great declaration of commitment from Moses' successor and the leader of Israel has been the motto for generations of Christian families, being displayed proudly in countless homes.

There isn't a better motto for a family to adopt. Joshua made a courageous, deliberate, and determined commitment to lead his family in the worship and service of the true God, the Lord God of Israel. The interesting thing is that Joshua was making this commitment not only for his immediate family but on behalf of generations yet to come.

We know this because the events recorded in Joshua 24 were Joshua's last acts as Israel's leader. Just before he died (v. 29), Joshua gathered the people of Israel together at the edge of Canaan for a final exhortation. He was aware of the spiritual dangers that lay ahead for Israel among the idolatrous Canaanites, and also the Israelites' own tendency to stray from the Lord. So he put the choice to them in the clearest possible terms:

> *Now therefore fear the LORD and serve him in sincerity and in faithfulness. Put away the gods that your fathers served beyond the River and in Egypt, and serve the LORD. And if it is evil in your eyes to serve the LORD, choose this day whom you will serve, whether the gods your fathers served in the region beyond the River, or the gods of the Amorites in whose land you dwell. But as for me and my house, we will serve the LORD. (vv. 14-15)*

It was in this setting that Joshua took his stand of faithfulness to God. Joshua left no room for neutrality or equivocation, because he knew that if the Israelites did not choose *for* God, they were choosing *against* Him. This was courageous leadership from a man who loved God and wanted his family and the future generations of Israel to love and serve God with all their hearts. Let's consider what it takes for us to make the same courageous commitment today and make it stick.

We Must Be Committed to Instill Godly Traits in Our Children

We've heard a lot of talk about the importance of character lately as business executives, athletes, politicians, and other public figures continue to tumble from the spotlight amid charges of dishonesty and misconduct. While this book was being written, the CEO of a large corporation in Ft. Worth resigned after it was revealed he had not received the college degree that he had listed on his résumé.

Since God is the ultimate builder of true character that passes the tests of time and temptation, we need to consult His Word to know what traits and values go into forming godly character in our children, so they will be able to stand for the Lord as Joshua did in the middle of a confused and evil generation.

As we raised our children, and as grandparents who are excited to be part of a new generation in our family, we jotted down six areas of character that we believe are crucial to instill in your children. We hope they will give you some steps to help mark the path in the all-important task of parenting.

Instill Confidence in Your Children

As parents we want our children to be confident in the sense of being secure in who they are in our family, and especially who they are in Jesus Christ. The best statement of this confidence is Paul's declaration, "I can do all things through [Christ] who strengthens me" (Philippians 4:13). This was not a boast but a testimony of confidence in God.

Jack: When our children were growing up, I would sometimes drop them off at school, a party, or some other function and tell them, "Remember who you are and whose you are." I wasn't just reminding them that they were members of the Graham family, although that was important. I was reminding them that they were members of God's family too. Deb and I never wanted our kids to doubt that they were secure in our love and in our home and in Christ.

One key to raising confident children is to express your confidence in them to do the right thing and make good choices. Many things are wrong with the approach being taken to the issue of teen sexuality by groups like Planned Parenthood and the public schools. The basic approach is to say to young people, "Look, we know you are going to have sex anyway because you can't control yourselves, so the best thing you can do is use a condom and practice safe sex."

It would take a chapter in itself to deal with the lack of morality in this mind-set. But one of the really damaging effects of this approach is the incredibly low level of expectation it communicates to young people and a complete lack of confidence in their ability to exercise self-control. And don't think kids aren't getting the message that we adults don't expect much from them.

Instill Conviction in Your Children

Polls continue to indicate that the majority of Americans do not believe in the concept of absolute truth. This includes many people who claim the name of Christ and are church members. The old saying is that people who don't believe anything will fall for everything. Those words could be written across the forehead of this generation, and one result is that we are producing people who are determined not to take a firm stand for anything for fear of being labeled intolerant.

But truth by its nature *is* intolerant—not of people, but of that which is false. Help your children and grandchildren understand that God has given us the truth in the person of Jesus Christ. John wrote: "Truth came through Jesus Christ" (John 1:17). Truth always demands a decision on our part, and one of the best things you can do for your children is to help them know what they believe and why they believe it and to encourage them to stand on their convictions no matter what.

Some people think we need to wait until our kids are older to deal with "heavy" issues such as truth. But there are two problems with that approach. First, children form their basic attitudes and beliefs at a very young age. Those whose job it is to indoctrinate people into their way of thinking have known this fact for years. Truth is too important to wait. And second, Satan as the master deceiver is constantly pouring lies into the minds of our children. Satan doesn't wait until they're teenagers to try and capture their minds.

What's the answer? You need to indoctrinate your children in the truth. Indoctrination sounds like bad news to those of us who grew up in the Cold War era when Communism was battling for the minds of the world. But look at the word again and you'll see that the heart of it is "doctrine." Doctrine is simply what the Bible teaches. Those truths need to be instilled into our kids until they become settled convictions. And truth instilled becomes truth lived out.

We wanted our children to grow up with firm convictions that were grounded in the Word of God, not simply with opinions or preferences. We prayed that they would not settle for convenient truth that is practiced when it's convenient, comfortable truth that is practiced when it's comfortable, or cultural truth that is practiced only until the times change. We wanted them to be filled with convictional truth that comes from God.

Instill Character in Your Children

One product of deep-seated convictions is solid character. Truth transforms character, so much so that there is no character without conviction. We parents really need to come to grips with the fact that if all we do is give our kids rules without building convictions in them, what we get is outward conformity with no inward character, which lasts only as long as the kids are under our authority. "Do it because I'm the parent and I say so" doesn't work in the long run if we don't back the "say so" with the reasons why some things are right and others are wrong.

This lack of character is why some young people become completely different once they are away from home. This often comes out most noticeably when they go away to college. Ask college students at your church if they have seen this phenomenon happen with other students in their dorm, and they will probably be able to tell you about someone they know.

One case we heard about involved a Christian young woman who went to a large state university in Texas. As her parents were helping her move in, they met her roommate and her parents, who were from a small farming community near the school. They said the roommate seemed like a very sweet, shy young lady who was just excited to have the chance to go to college.

But almost as soon as her parents drove away, this farm girl morphed into a wild partygoer and heavy drinker who stayed out all weekend and brought a guy into the room. She also started hiding alcohol in their room, a violation that would have resulted in both girls being expelled, no questions asked. The Christian roommate and her family were distraught trying to figure out what to do since the dorms were full and she couldn't change roommates. Thankfully, she was able to get through the semester and the other girl eventually flunked out as her grades went south while she was living it up.

All parents wonder at times how their children will act once they are away from the house, and that concern doesn't begin in college. One nervous mother ran up to her child's kindergarten teacher on the first "Meet the Teacher" night and blurted out, "I'm Johnny Smith's mother. Please tell me, will I be bragging or complaining?"

Instilling character in our children doesn't mean they won't ever venture off the path or try things they shouldn't. But having well-rooted character gives children and young adults an inner sense of conviction to which the Holy Spirit can appeal in drawing them toward the right. When your children not only know the difference between right and wrong but have the courage to stand for the right even when no one is looking, you have produced a person of character.

Instill Compassion in Your Children

All caring begins in the heart, with true compassion for those who are hurting. As Jesus told the story we know as the Parable of the Good Samaritan, He said that when the Samaritan came upon the man lying bleeding and wounded by the side of the road, "He had compassion" on him (Luke 10:33).

Compassionate parents produce compassionate children. Take your kids with you as you go out to serve the needy in your church and community. There is certainly no lack of opportunities to care for others; it's just a matter of getting up and going where the needs are.

Being compassionate requires turning away from self-indulgence and self-centeredness. You often hear complaints about teenagers whose lives seem to revolve around their cell phones and the mall. But we want to tell you that we are encouraged by what we see happening in the lives of teenagers and young adults in our church and in other churches. They are going to the mission field at home and abroad, pouring their hearts and lives into hurting people, demonstrating and sharing the love of Christ. There's nothing more exciting than to watch your children grow into people of compassion.

Jack: I had the amazing adventure of taking Kelly with me on a mission trip to Honduras with Samaritan's Purse relief organization. We shared some wonderful days of ministering in small poverty-stricken villages in the mountains. I can still remember seeing Kelly holding a small child, loving her, and telling her about Jesus. My heart swelled with joy. It was just the beginning of seeing Kelly's heart for children. She continues to this day sponsoring youth groups in mission work. She is an amazing communicator and uses her second language of Spanish whenever presented the opportunity.

Parents often say, "I want to give my children what I didn't have." Well, that's OK as long as you don't forget to give them what you *did* have. If you were raised to care about people, pass that compassion along to your children, and watch them make a difference in the world for Jesus Christ.

Instill Competence in Your Children

We need to raise competent children. Part of this is teaching them how to do the everyday things of life well, whether it's learning how to handle money or carrying out their chores at home with excellence.

One dad had a great plan for making sure his teenage son was competent to take the car out on his first date. This dad had his son drive them on the route he was going to take that evening. This family lived in a large city, so the dad wanted to be sure his son knew the right exits and so forth.

Once they had the route down and were on their way home, the dad said, "Son, you just had a flat tire."

"I don't think so, Dad," his son replied. "The car seems to be handling fine."

"No, son, you don't understand. You just had a flat tire. Pull over." The teenager had to get out right there and change the tire, which as his dad suspected he didn't know how to do. That mock exercise became a learning experience because a caring dad didn't want his son to have a flat tire on his date and be stranded with another dad's daughter in his care.

Of course, the competence our children need goes well beyond money management and car care to the spiritual gifts and abilities with which God has endowed them. You have the privilege of helping your children discover and use their spiritual gifts. It's also important to provide them with opportunities to develop their gifts because we are usually successful and fulfilled when we are serving in the areas of our giftedness—and that builds confidence and competence.

Philippians 4:13 bears repeating here: "I can do all things through [Christ] who strengthens me." God-instilled confidence leads to God-instilled competence as our children learn that in the power of the Holy Spirit they can do what God has gifted and called them to do.

Instill Love for the Church in Your Children

We love the church of Jesus Christ that He loves and died for, and we wanted our children to love the church. Regular church attendance is one area of Christian discipline that should be a must in any child's life. Being part of a local body of believers is not only a scriptural act of obedience (Hebrews 10:24-25), but it is a great bonding time for families.

PUTTING THE PLAN TO WORK

Deb: Our children have attended church since the day they were born. All of them were in church nurseries, Bible study classes, choirs, and mission organizations. We have been in churches of all sizes, and sometimes it may have seemed that we lived at the church. We went through everything from "separation anxiety" at the toddler stage to the "it's boring" stage of the kids' teen years. But there was never any discussion about where they would be when it was church time. They were with us, and that settled the matter. And those experiences of worship and fellowship helped make our children what they are today.

As each child became old enough to attend "big church," I tried to stay creative in keeping them occupied. With each passing year we graduated from coloring books, stickers, and Bible crosswords to actually taking sermon notes. Each child had his or her own way of making it through the service.

All of our children will tell you that they did not escape their dad's eye, even when he was preaching. And in some cases they heard their names called from the pulpit if they were misbehaving. Our sons vividly remember the horror of knowing that to be corrected at church was nothing compared to what awaited them at home.

But all in all, our family's times in church are among my fondest memories. I can still see Josh, our youngest son, and his little friend Aaron eagerly running into the worship center for the Sunday evening service. Josh would always take off his shoes and socks because he was a Florida boy who was used to beach life.

The boys would spend the first part of the service drawing pictures on the back of the offering envelopes and then usually stretch out on the pew between their mothers and fall fast asleep. (Those minutes of calm were refreshment not only to the boys but to everyone in the pews behind and in front of them!)

Jack's custom was to finish the service with an upbeat song; so the worship leader would often ask the congregation for a favorite chorus. At that precise moment our little redheaded Josh and his blond buddy

Aaron would suddenly sit up as if a firecracker had gone off and call out their favorite song, "What a Mighty God We Serve."

The congregation became accustomed to seeing two barefoot boys jump to their feet on the pews and begin to bounce up and down, singing that chorus at the top of their lungs. Their smiling faces, fresh from their naps, glowed with innocence and enthusiasm.

Now Josh and Aaron are young adults, college graduates with jobs in the business world. They are still involved in church and are still friends. Recently I asked them if they remembered those Sunday night services and "What a Mighty God We Serve." They both smiled, and you could tell it was a part of the seed that we had planted.

There will be times in all our children's lives when it would be easier on us to let them stay home from church, quit the team, or drop out of some other commitment they'd made. But in the end the things we believe in are not optional.

The greatest disservice a parent can do is to be halfhearted about anything in the Christian life, including our involvement with church. I urge you to make church attendance deliberate and purposeful for your family. Use every opportunity to nurture your children's spiritual gifts by giving them diverse and regular spiritual stimulation.

The greatest thing our parents did for Jack and me was to take us to church. It instilled in both of us a love for the church and for God's people that is still alive today and by God's grace will live on after us in our children and grandchildren.

BOTH PARENTS MUST BE COMMITTED TO TAKE A STAND FOR THE FAMILY

Instilling godly character in your children is the best way we know to make good on a commitment to take a stand for righteousness in your home. But at least two other facets of Joshua 24:15 are worth pointing out.

The first of these is the importance of full participation on the part of both parents. Joshua spoke in the plural when he said, "As for me and my house, *we* will serve the Lord" (emphasis added). Too many parents want to have children, but they fail to make a commitment to raise those children in the nurture and instruction of the Lord. Judging by the way some families operate, the parents must think children raise themselves.

But we hope the message is coming through loud and clear that children require the active participation, interest, and involvement of both parents at every stage of life. One of the most enlightening moments for parents of teenagers comes the day they realize their teens need them at least as much as, if not more than, they did when they were younger. The nature of parental involvement certainly changes with teenagers, but the basic fact never changes that our children need our time in massive doses. There is no substitute for our presence in their lives. God never intended for children to be raised by baby-sitters, nannies, schoolteachers, day-care workers, or relatives.

There are exceptions to this, of course. But the exceptions prove the rule. The tremendous strain that child care puts on single parents, grandparents, or other caregivers who have to be brought into the picture when a parent is missing—to say nothing of the strain on the children themselves—serves to demonstrate the wisdom of God's original plan for families. And He will hold us accountable for the stewardship of our children.

The message to couples who like having children but don't like taking care of them is this: it's time for you to reevaluate your priorities and your lifestyle if you are not giving your children the time they need. Our generation has more discretionary time than our parents had, but we are using it mostly for ourselves.

You can microwave dinner, but you can't microwave children into maturity. That takes lots of effort and energy. The real problem in our society is not delinquent children but drop-out dads and distracted moms who have their priorities out of whack.

You may be saying at this point, "Are you trying to make me feel guilty about not spending time with my kids?" If that's a problem for you, then the answer is yes!

Please understand, the idea is not just to produce guilt. But we are so passionate about parenting and so concerned about the disintegration of families that we're not afraid to shake things up and stir you to stop and think and examine your priorities if it will help you strengthen your commitment to raise godly children.

Sometimes we as Christians are so concerned about not offending anyone or just being nice that we become passé about issues about which we should be passionate. One recent example of this came over the airwaves on one of our local Christian radio stations. The host was interviewing a family expert who shared the shocking numbers about the miniscule amount of time the average father spends with his children each week.

We've cited those figures, but what was interesting was the way this family expert, who is part of a wonderful Christian ministry, prefaced his statement: "Now we don't want to put anyone on a guilt trip here, but . . ." Then he cited the figures on dads' lack of involvement with their kids.

The speaker's caution is understandable because he was a guest on that radio program. But let's get real for a minute. If the numbers are really that bad, and if kids all over America—including kids in Christian homes—are basically growing up without much input from their fathers, *someone* had better be taking a guilt trip and doing something about the problem!

Who are we kidding? If you've ever tried standing on one leg for long, you know how hard it is to keep your balance. That's why God gave us two legs. It's the same with parenting. God gave our children two parents, and it takes both parents standing together to keep the home in balance.

WE MUST BE COMMITTED TO TAKE A STAND FOR FUTURE GENERATIONS

We pointed out earlier that Joshua was speaking about the future generations of his family when he took his stand and said, "We will serve the LORD."

The Bible says, "Blessed is the man who fears the LORD, who greatly delights in his commandments! His offspring will be mighty in the land; the generation of the upright will be blessed" (Psalm 112:1-2).

These verses are both a prayer that we might be parents who are "upright" in God's sight and a promise that when we are faithful to our calling, God will bless the future generations of our families. By faith we can look down the tunnel of time and see our children, grandchildren, and great-grandchildren knowing and loving Jesus Christ in part because of the godly heritage we have established.

Jack: I was scared as a young pastor entering the ministry because I'd seen a lot of preachers before me lose their kids while trying to win others. I knew that Jesus asked us, "What will it profit a man if he gains the whole world, and loses his own soul?" (Mark 8:36, NKJV). So I asked myself, *What will it profit a pastor if he wins the whole world and loses his own family?*

With that challenge before me, I made some decisions early in my ministry about the time I would set aside for Deb and my children, because my overriding ambition is that my family will love and serve Jesus in every generation. I encourage you to take a look down that tunnel of time and begin praying a prayer something like this: "O God, start a fire in me of passionate love and devotion for You that will not be put out as long as my family is on this earth."

Prior generations did that for us, and now it's our turn to pass the torch of faith on to future generations. And the time is short.

When we were young parents, older parents used to tell us, "Pay attention to your kids because the years are going to pass just like that." And like a lot of young parents, we pretty much said, "Yeah, yeah," thinking to ourselves, *We have a long time.*

But now we're the older parents, and we can tell you, the time you have with your children will fly by! Don't wake up one day and say, "I wish I had it to do all over again." Do it right starting today!

That's the great thing about parenting. It comes with adjustable controls. Realize that God gave you children not just because He wants more people out there who look and act like you, but because He wants more people who look and act like Jesus. We are raising our children not just to bear our name but to bear the name of Jesus Christ. Not just to make a name for ourselves but to make a name for the Lord our God.

So draw a line at the front door of your home, and take your stand with Joshua and other godly parents. Then one day when your family is gathered around the throne of God in heaven, your greatest joy will be to report, "Lord, we're all here."

7

HOMELAND
SECURITY

YOU CAN STOP almost any person on any street in America and get the correct answer to the question, "When did the phrase *homeland security* become a familiar part of our national vocabulary?"

Except perhaps for someone who has been stranded on a remote island for the past few years, most Americans can tell you that homeland security became a part of our national life following the 9/11 terror attacks. A 9/11 Commission was set up to investigate the attacks and decide what could be done to prevent future attacks. Soon afterward the Department of Homeland Security was established.

According to one government web site, the Bush administration provided the 9/11 Commission with unprecedented access to White House personnel and documents. This included nearly a thousand interviews with administration officials and an unbelievable total of 2.3 *million* pages of documents that were made available for the Commission's review.

With a dangerous enemy out there waiting to strike if we let down our guard, few dispute the importance of the attention that America is giving to maintaining homeland security. Protecting the home front is important in the spiritual realm as well because we too have an enemy out there who is waiting to strike. The Bible cautions us about him: "Be sober-minded; be watchful. Your adversary the devil prowls around like a roaring lion, seeking someone to devour" (1 Peter 5:8).

The devil is not a cartoon character or a Halloween figure running around in a red suit and a pitchfork. He is a relentless, devouring enemy, and the ones he is most eager to devour are our children. But the Lord has given us a powerful homeland security plan in His Word, and He has appointed us as parents to be the administrators of this plan. What is required to maintain your family's homeland security?

HOMELAND SECURITY REQUIRES A FAMILY WITH INTEGRITY

Remember your high school math? We learned that an integer is a whole number. That's the core of the word *integrity*, which means to be whole or complete. A good military defense is one that doesn't have any large holes or gaps in it where the enemy can find a weak spot and punch through. Likewise, a family that wants to practice good spiritual homeland security needs to close any gaps in its defense and stand on alert together as a complete unit.

Family Integrity Begins with the Covenant of Marriage

We have a portrait of a family that has integrity, or wholeness, in Ephesians 6:1-4. There we read that a family of integrity is one in which children are in obedience to parents who love them and nurture them in the things of God.

This family portrait actually begins in verses 22-33 of chapter 5, which describes a husband and wife joined together in loving commitment to one another and to Christ in the covenant of marriage. This is where the foundation of the family is laid. God established both the institution and the order of the home in the beginning when He created the human race as "male and female" (Genesis 1:27) and ordained that these two would be joined together in marriage as one flesh (Genesis 2:24).

Our culture desperately needs to recover the concept of marriage as a lifelong covenant, not as something you get a license to do the way you go get a license to drive a car. A covenant is a binding agreement, a commitment that all parties involved will faithfully keep its terms.

────────

Jack: I think it's important for us to understand that God was a party to the key covenants made in the Bible. For example, God made a covenant with Noah after the Flood in which He promised never again to destroy the earth by water (Genesis 9:8-17). Later God made a covenant with Abram (Genesis 15:7-21) that He would give the land of Canaan to him and his descendants, the Jews, forever. God also made a covenant with David (2 Samuel 7:12-16) that stipulated that David's house and throne would be established forever—a promise that will be fully and finally realized when Jesus Christ comes again to rule on the throne of David. In fact, all three of these covenants are still in effect today.

My point is that a biblical covenant is not just a private agreement between two or more people. The Lord is part of the agreement, and He expects faithfulness to His covenant. The reason preachers invoke God as a witness to a Christian wedding is not because that's what it says to do in the marriage manual, but because He is as real a party to a marriage as are the bride and groom. Viewing your marriage as a covenant relationship made with your spouse and with God takes it to a whole new level of importance.

So solid family defense begins with the right people in the right place. A dad and mom who are in a growing love relationship with each other and with Christ are the first line of defense in providing homeland security for their family.

────────

Deb: My heart goes out to single parents who are working so hard to provide for their families while trying to fill the gap left by the missing partner. Single-parent families can be families of integrity too as they rely on the Lord to provide the spiritual wholeness that is possible even if one of the marriage partners is not there.

That certainly doesn't mean it will be easy for single parents. But this is where the church can be such a great help and support to God's people. Our church has a wonderful ministry to single-parent families that is designed to be an arm of support for these parents to lean on. If you are a single parent, Jack and I urge you to seek out godly men and women in your church who can be an encouragement to you and an example to your children.

We Must Be Ready to Fight for the Integrity of Our Family

In Psalm 11:3 the psalmist asked a penetrating question: "If the foundations are destroyed, what can the righteous do?" Most Bible commentators agree that this is a reference to the laws and order of society that God established. We are seeing those foundations of our society being undermined in ways that the previous generation could never have imagined, and the enemy is concentrating his heaviest attacks on the family.

We saw what happened when the foundations of the city of New Orleans, the levees that held back the sea, were destroyed by Hurricane Katrina in August 2005. The city was rendered completely vulnerable to the raging waters that took away homes and lives.

The raging waters of divorce and family breakup, the push to legalize same-sex marriage, the disregard of marriage by couples living together, and the celebration of dysfunctional families by the entertainment media are all pounding away at the foundations of the family. We're in a battle to preserve the integrity of our homes. We've gone from *Ozzie and Harriet* of a previous generation to *Ozzie and the Osbournes.* Mercifully, this latter program didn't last for too many seasons, but plenty of other reality shows out there present incredibly mixed-up messages about the family. And instead of shocking us, they have become the standard for many people.

Earlier we mentioned Ephesians 6:1-4, where children are told to obey their parents and parents are told to raise their children "in the discipline and instruction of the Lord" (v. 4). It's important to see that this beautiful picture of a family with integrity is set in a context of spiritual warfare. The apostle Paul went on to say:

Finally, be strong in the Lord and in the strength of his might. Put on the whole armor of God, that you may be able to stand against the schemes of the devil. For we do not wrestle against flesh and blood, but against the rulers, against the authorities, against the cosmic powers over this present darkness, against the spiritual forces of evil in the heavenly places. Therefore take up the whole armor of God, that you may be able to withstand in the evil day, and having done all, to stand firm. (vv. 10-13)

In the following verses the Bible gives us the armor of God that we need to put on and take up so we can defend ourselves and our families against the enemy's attacks. There are some things worth fighting for—and the family is worth the fight at every level, from the White House and the statehouse to your house. Thankfully, a number of members of Congress and other leaders are alert to the fact that if the foundations of the family crumble, our civilization will be in deep trouble. They are leading the fight for an amendment to the Constitution to protect marriage, and they need our support in this battle.

Integrity Demands That We Set High Standards

Sometimes evangelical Christians who believe God's Word are accused of worshiping the idea of family, making it the be-all and end-all as if it's the solution to every problem in our society. Our goal certainly is not to worship the family, nor are we suggesting that having a family is a guarantee of an idyllic life. There are many broken families in which lives have been shattered, and part of the church's calling is to help these people put the pieces back together again.

But while we don't want to worship the family, we do want to hold God's standards high in our generation. The reality of imperfect and broken families only makes it more important than ever that we fight to maintain God's ideal as the standard toward which every family should be striving. Lowering the standard doesn't help people who are struggling. It just makes it easier for other people to settle for less than God's best in their families.

Contrary to popular opinion, marriage done God's way is not an antique concept that has outlived its usefulness and needs to be replaced by other options more suited to our modern culture. Marriage God's way is the only way to preserve and protect our families and children—and ultimately our very civilization. While our nation is implementing homeland security to defend ourselves against those who want to destroy our way of life, we as parents had better be sure we are providing our children with security on the home front by making our marriages and homes places where love rules and Christ reigns.

Deb: A couple of years ago, after Jack had been elected president of the Southern Baptist Convention, our family and friends held a little celebration for us. During the evening the hosts asked our children—Jason and his wife Toby, our daughter Kelly, and our younger son Josh—to say a word about their father. One of the comments that Jason made referred to his dad's commitment to our marriage as a lifelong partnership.

Jason said to Jack, "I remember as a little boy we were watching an episode of *The Love Boat* on television, and something came up about divorce. I had never heard that word before and didn't know what it meant, so I asked you, 'Daddy what's divorce?' You explained to me what divorce meant, but the thing I remember about that night is what you said next: 'Jason, you'll never have to worry about divorce in this family because I'm committed to your mother and I'm going to be faithful to her my whole life.' Tonight I just want to thank you and Mom for being faithful to each other."

Jack: You can imagine what it meant to both Deb and me to hear Jason say that. Deb deserves the lion's share of the credit for our home, but hearing Jason express his gratitude for the security he felt as a little boy in our family was far more important to me than being elected to the presidency of our convention. In fact, knowing that our children grew up in the stability and strength of a home where Mom and Dad were committed to each other means more to me than any accomplishment I could achieve in the ministry.

What we're saying is that the family is worth fighting for. And this is truly a winnable war because we are fighting from a position of victory. One of the most encouraging statements in the Bible comes right in the middle of a section of Scripture in which Paul was writing about the challenges, heartaches, and tests of ministry. Despite these things, he exclaimed with joy, "Thanks be to God, who in Christ always leads us in triumphal procession" (2 Corinthians 2:14). Jesus won the victory on the cross. All we need to do is collect the spoils.

Knowing that the battle for our families is a worthy and winnable battle should give us new strength for the struggle. One thing that every husband and wife can do for their family is to stay together. We used to hear that it was damaging to the children for a couple to stay together if they were having a bad time in their marriage. But if, as family experts tell us, divorce is even harder emotionally on children than the death of a parent, then we have to ask, what could be worse for a family than to split up?

Now don't misunderstand. We're not saying that two people in a troubled marriage need to just stay that way for the rest of their lives with no attempt to get help. But we are saying that as long as both parties in a marriage are still breathing, there is hope for restoration and reconciliation that preserves the wholeness, the *integrity*, of the family. For the sake of your children as well as your own well-being, as much as it is within your power don't allow anything to destroy the security of your home.

HOMELAND SECURITY REQUIRES A FAMILY TO SET BOUNDARIES

Since the war on terror began after 9/11, we have been witnessing the truth of an old phrase that our parents knew very well: "Freedom isn't free." Families all across this country have paid a terrible price for freedom in the loss of a child, spouse, or parent.

The truth is that freedom has never been free. The freedom we have in Christ cost our Savior His life. Freedom always comes with a price, and it always has boundaries to it. One of the biggest myths in the world is that freedom means being free to do whatever you want, whenever you want to do it. The Bible cautions us, "For you were called to freedom, brothers. Only do not use your freedom as an opportunity for the flesh, but through love serve one another" (Galatians 5:13).

Boundaries Give Children a Strong Sense of Security

One of the greatest favors you can do for your children is to set firm boundaries that clearly mark the path they are to take. This means more than doing them a favor. Parents are given the command to raise their children "in the discipline and instruction of the Lord" (Ephesians 6:4). Among other things, this speaks of setting limits and boundaries on their behavior. Boundaries are a necessary part of practicing spiritual homeland security because our children experience a tremendous sense of security when they know where the lines are.

This doesn't mean that our children are going to come to us and say, "Thank you, Father and Mother, for setting firm boundaries for us. We appreciate you so much for expressing your love for us in this way." If your children say that to you anytime before they become adults and/or parents themselves, you need to write a book on how you did it!

More likely, your experience will be the same as most parents because children love to test the limits of their freedom. We are all born with an instinctive desire to be free of restraints and follow our own desires. It's called the sin nature, and we came by it honestly from our parents, who got it from their parents and so on all the way back to Adam.

Part of skillful parenting is helping children enjoy true freedom within the boundaries that God has set for us in His Word. One of the classic strategies of military defense is to set up a perimeter around an encampment in order to detect and stop the encroaching enemy before they reach the heart of your camp. The troops are usually safe to move about within the perimeter, which is ringed with weapons and guards.

But when the troops move outside the perimeter, they understand that they have left the protection of the camp and are in hostile territory.

Most of us experienced the blessing of boundaries without realizing it when we were kids playing games, whether it was an outdoor game or a board game in the living room. It seems like one kid always suddenly tried to change the rules when it was to his advantage, while all the other kids howled in protest. Childhood games are a great way to learn we can't get anywhere without rules and boundaries.

Make Your Home's Rules Few and Firm

Some parents might read this and say, "OK, we get it. Since we need to set boundaries for our children, we'll just make a bunch of rules to govern every part of their lives so they'll always know exactly where to go and what to do."

Actually, we recommend that you go light on the number of rules. One reason is to keep from frustrating your children, which is part of your biblical admonition as parents. The Bible says, "Do not provoke your children to anger," and "Do not provoke your children, lest they become discouraged" (Ephesians 6:4; Colossians 3:21). Nothing frustrates children faster than a long list of rules. Besides, the more rules you have, the more likely it is that some of them will be unreasonable.

Another reason to keep the house rules down to a few biggies is to keep from frustrating yourselves as the enforcers. We've all heard of the parents who say to their teenager in a moment of exasperation, "You're grounded for a month!" Later the parents realize they have just sentenced themselves and their child to thirty days of misery; so they either have to back off on their word and look weak or stick it out.

We had very few rules in our home—few enough for our children to remember them and to get the message that each one was important. For instance, being in God's house worshiping with God's people was an absolute priority in our house—and not just because Dad was the preacher. We took seriously the Bible's command not to forsake "the assembling of ourselves together" (Hebrews 10:25, NKJV). We love the church and are committed to it, and that priority came through in our rules.

Since our kids knew where they were expected to be when worship time came, that rule governed a lot of the decisions they made about various activities and saved us from being bombarded with a lot of questions such as "Can we go here?" or "Can we do this or that?" They knew that if something interfered with worship, it was out. Of course, there were times when we needed to consider the circumstances, but in general the rule stood firm, and everyone knew it.

Well-known speaker Josh McDowell often says that rules without relationship leads to rebellion. We tried to base our parenting more on relationships than on rules. We wanted our children to obey not just out of fear that they would get it if they messed up but because they loved and respected us and knew we had their best interests at heart.

And by the way, that's a level of maturity we as believers need to come to in our relationship with God. It's amazing how many adult Christians are still relating to God on the basis of the fear of punishment instead of obeying Him out of love. A lot of people learned that fear pattern of relating when they were children because they grew up in homes that were heavy on the rules and punishment but thin on love and relationships.

Setting Boundaries Rules Out Being Passive or Permissive

There is always the danger that some parents will interpret few rules and lots of relationship as a call to be either passive or permissive with their children. But the exact opposite is true. No matter how few or how many rules you have, setting and enforcing them requires active parenting.

Passive parents are those who simply don't care what their kids do or with whom they do it. A friend told us about a family in his neighborhood in Florida where the parents used to lock their five children out of the house for hours on end. Even if the kids wanted to ask permission to go to someone else's house to play or ride their bikes to the store, they couldn't because their dad threatened mayhem if they disturbed the parents before the time he had announced.

This was in the late fifties and early sixties when there wasn't the fear for child safety there is today. So the kids in this family would wander around the neighborhood like orphans, looking for a place to hang out until it was OK to go home.

Passive parents are a problem, but permissive parents may be worse. We're talking about the kind of parents who not only allow but in some cases *enable* their children to engage in destructive behavior. One of the growing trends in permissive parenting is parent-sponsored drinking parties in their homes, at which teenagers are furnished with alcohol. These parents' philosophy is, "Our kids are going to drink anyway, so we would rather provide the alcohol for them at our house in a controlled environment than have them out drinking and driving around."

Jesus said of a person who causes a child to stumble, "It would be better for him if a millstone were hung around his neck and he were cast into the sea than that he should cause one of these little ones to sin" (Luke 17:2). Obviously, parents who help their children drink in violation of the law and the standards of morality are the extreme example of permissiveness. But any time we are permissive where we should be setting a high standard, we are failing our children.

Set reasonable boundaries for your children, and take the time to enforce them. Children who are not disciplined feel unloved and insecure. Discipline says to a child, "I love you too much to let you live life without limits."

Deb: Having three children over a span of ten years gave us a good sampling of temperaments, and each of our children needed discipline and correction in a different way. As the oldest, Jason provided a strong role model for the other two. Having Kelly added some tears to our strong male household, and Josh, our red-haired baby, always "got away with murder," the other two would frequently say.

I remember one day when Jack was administering a much-needed dose of correction to Jason and Kelly, who were about thirteen and nine years of age at the time. Being the disciplinarian that he was, Jack had both of them up in our bedroom on the second floor of our house in Florida to face the music.

I was summoned to the bedroom while Jack read them the riot act and said this type of behavior was not going to be tolerated. After the appropriate reprimand both were asked if they were ever going to do the deed again. As Kelly sobbed out her answer that she would never do such a thing again, we heard clunky footsteps coming down the hall. Jack turned to find three-year-old Josh standing at the bedroom door, dressed in full football regalia. "And what do you have to say for yourself, young man?" Jack asked him.

Josh's big brown eyes sparkled from under the large helmet as he shouted excitedly, "I'm a Dallas Cowboy!" We looked at each other and then turned quickly away as we burst out laughing. Even at his young age, Josh already knew that his dad loved football, especially the Dallas Cowboys, and he figured out that coming as a Cowboy would spare him the rod.

When he saw us laughing, Josh jumped up and down and said again, "I'm a Dallas Cowboy!" We all had a big hug and piled on Josh for a good tickle. For years to come, every time the children stood before us to receive correction I envisioned that three-year-old in his football uniform, his eyes flashing under the oversized helmet.

HOMELAND SECURITY REQUIRES A FAMILY THAT BLESSES

This is the other side of the coin of setting boundaries. In the Scripture, the blessing of a father was one of the most important moments in the life of a child. It was the affirmation of God's hand on the child's life and was passed from generation to generation. The blessing was a formal event in the ancient world and was so coveted that Jacob was willing to cheat his father Isaac and his brother Esau to get it for himself (Genesis 27).

Later, as Jacob fled from Esau's anger, God appeared to Jacob in a dream and blessed him (Genesis 28:12-16). Jacob was so aware of the power of a blessing that he made this plea to the man who wrestled with him in another famous incident: "I will not let you go unless you bless me!" (Genesis 32:26).

Bless Your Children with Words of Affirmation

Boundaries provide the security of saying to your children, "This is the area within which you are safe to move." A *blessing* provides the security of saying, "We love you and see God's unique hand of blessing on your life. You are His child, and He is going to bless you and use your gifts and talents in incredible ways."

You may not say words like these to your child, but that's the message a blessing conveys. When children are younger, your blessing may be simply a hug and an "I love you." More and more parents are taking the opportunity to pass on a formal blessing to their children at an occasion such as a graduation or wedding, and we encourage you to consider it.

Some parents write letters to their kids or write down thoughts in a journal and then present those to their children at the appropriate time. However you share your blessing, you can't imagine how powerful your words of affirmation are to your children.

Sometimes children inadvertently give us hints about how much these things mean to them. You've probably had the experience of telling your kids a story about something that happened in your family, and one of the kids will say something like, "Really? Wow! I never knew that. That's cool." What they're telling you is that they want to know.

Times like these are reminders that your blessing can go beyond individual affirmation to each child. It's also important to pass on stories of God's blessing on your family. A best-selling book on great companies written some years ago said that storytelling is one trait of such companies. The author said great companies make sure their employees know the stories of their company's success in getting started, encouraging growth, and so on. This storytelling had a very positive effect because it helped the employees realize they were part of something historic and exciting, and they were more motivated to live up to the company's great history and reputation.

If we had to guess, we would say that most families, and especially fathers, are better at setting boundaries than at passing on a blessing.

Many children grow up hearing only negative words. One boy said, "I thought my name was 'Shut up' for the first six years of my life."

———

Jack: Blessing our children is an area of real passion for me, both as a father and as a pastor to many fathers. Maybe you're hearing the alarms that are going off today about the crisis that boys are in. Boys are falling seriously behind girls in every area of emotional and intellectual development, and even some secular experts are realizing that our culture has been a toxic environment for boys for at least the past thirty years.

This phenomenon is often called the "feminizing" of boys, and people are wringing their hands over the problem. I don't have all the answers, but I know from God's Word that a father who blesses his children, and especially his sons, gives them a gift and a solid place to stand no matter what the culture dishes out.

Bless Your Children with a Knowledge of the Word

The greatest blessing your children will ever know is when you open God's Word with them and help them understand how much God loves them and how He made them as His unique treasure. The Bible says, "Faith comes by hearing, and hearing by the word of God" (Romans 10:17, NKJV). That's not just a great verse for evangelism, but a great word to parents.

If you want your children to be strong and secure in this world, fill them up with God's truth. Partner with your church in making sure that your children are learning, living, and loving the Bible. We don't know where the events of life will take our children or what winds of culture will blow over them in the days ahead. But we can anchor them in God's Word and cling to this promise: "The grass withers, the flower fades, but the word of our God will stand forever" (Isaiah 40:8).

8

WILL THE REAL PARENTS PLEASE STAND UP?

YOU MAY REMEMBER *To Tell the Truth*, the old television panel show in which three contestants claimed to be the same person and tried to fool the panel with their story. After the panel had voted, the host would say in a slow fashion, "Will the real . . . John Jones . . . please . . . stand up!" The contestants would shuffle in their chairs and look at each other, and then the real person would finally stand up.

Today it seems as if many parents have forgotten who they are and what they are supposed to be doing. And the area where parents are missing in action perhaps more than any other is in the formation of their children's sexual attitudes, values, and behavior. And unfortunately we have to admit that in many cases Christian families aren't faring much better than families in the world.

But we're convinced that Christian parents want to have a strong, positive influence on their children's moral and sexual attitudes. They just need help, and we have the best resource possible in the timeless counsel of God's Word. The Scriptures can help us as we seek to guide our kids through the cultural minefield they have to walk through.

One of the best ways to learn how to do something is to ask someone who's been there ahead of us, has seen it all, and can warn us about the pitfalls and potholes in the road. We're going to do that as we arm ourselves for the task of giving our children clear moral guidance in a sex-saturated culture. The apostle Paul experienced a first-century society that was not only a lot like our twenty-first century in terms of moral decadence but was even worse in some ways.

He particularly faced this in the cosmopolitan city of Corinth, where Paul lived for about eighteen months as he helped establish the church there. Corinth was famous for its sexual corruption, and one definition of the adjective *Corinthian* is "a loose-living person." The Corinthians didn't have Internet porn available, but they did have sex on demand as prostitutes walked the streets decked out in gold jewelry and braided hair. And just about any sexual perversion could be satisfied at the temple where "sacred" prostitutes of both sexes plied their sin in the name of religion. Is any of this sounding familiar? The Corinthians stole a page out of our culture's playbook—or more likely it's the other way around.

Immoral, indecent, and immodest—that pretty well sums up Corinthian society. And many, if not most, of the Christians in the church at Corinth had been saved out of that very wicked lifestyle. We know that because Paul wrote:

> *Do not be deceived: neither the sexually immoral, nor idolaters, nor adulterers, nor men who practice homosexuality, nor thieves, nor the greedy, nor drunkards, nor revilers, nor swindlers will inherit the kingdom of God. And such were some of you. But you were washed, you were sanctified, you were justified in the name of the Lord Jesus Christ and by the Spirit of our God. (1 Corinthians 6:9-11)*

You can't name a city in America or the world that is worse than Corinth was. Paul's teaching to the church in Corinth concerning sexual purity is a message that transcends cultures and centuries because God's plan and human nature have not changed. The Bible's message is a radical call to purity and holiness and moral sanity in a sex-crazed, secularized culture. And the fact that the Corinthian believers were able to exist in that kind of setting and yet live holy lives means that God can give anyone the power to honor Him in the area of sexual morality.

The Bible gives us clear instructions and moral imperatives for the way we ought to live. We have touched on some of these issues before, but the goal in this chapter is to focus sharply on moral purity and to develop key principles that we first need to live out as parents and then pass on to our children.

Our main text is 1 Corinthians 6:15-20, which includes this unmistakable command: "Run away from sexual sin! No other sin so clearly affects the body as this one does. For sexual immorality is a sin against your own body" (v. 18, NLT). Here is a clear call to purity that is the place to start in helping our children live for Christ in a world that tries to turn them the other way.

TEACH YOUR CHILDREN THE PRIORITY OF PURITY

No one ever has to wonder what the Bible teaches about sexual sin: It's wrong every time, period. The word translated "sexual sin" (ESV: "sexual immorality") in 1 Corinthians 6:18 is *porneia*, from which comes the English word *pornography*. It's a reference to any sexual activity that is outside the bonds of marriage—sexual sin of all kinds, in other words. We are told to run from it because of the damage it does to our bodies and spirits, to say nothing of the fact that it displeases God. "Let marriage be held in honor among all, and let the marriage bed be undefiled, for God will judge the sexually immoral and adulterous" (Hebrews 13:4).

Why does God forbid sexual immorality? Because He has an infinitely better plan and purpose for human relationships. God is not against sex—He's for it. After all, He created it. What God is against is the perversion of His plan to bring a man and woman together in a covenantal, loving marriage relationship in which they can enjoy each other to the full. Sex isn't dirty but sacred. And like anything that is sacred, it is to be guarded and kept for its intended purpose. We need to help our children understand that God is not keeping sex *from* them but is keeping it *for* them to be expressed in the way He intended.

A real problem we fight as parents is that our kids are getting so much twisted misinformation from their peers about sex. One example is the idea that kids who refrain from having sex are missing out on fun and will wind up as old spinsters and bachelors who never got to experience love. From an adult standpoint we can see how silly that kind of thinking is. But droves of teenagers and preteens are believing this lie or some version of it and are making destructive decisions based on it.

Another lie that many of America's young people are buying into is the myth of so-called casual sex. College students and other young adults call it hooking up, a term for having multiple sex partners in unions that are meant to be temporary, random, and almost anonymous, with no thought whatsoever of intimacy or involvement on the part of the guy or girl.

The tragedy of this approach to sex is obvious from the way Paul described the true nature of sex earlier in 1 Corinthians 6: "Do you not know that your bodies are members of Christ? Shall I then take the members of Christ and make them members of a prostitute? Never! Or do you not know that he who is joined to a prostitute becomes one body with her? For, as it is written, 'The two will become one flesh.' But he who is joined to the Lord becomes one spirit with him" (vv. 15-17). These verses and the ones that follow are worth a closer look.

Sexual Sin Forms Bonds That Are Powerful and Destructive

Paul began at the right place, which is that as Christians our bodies don't belong to us to do whatever we want with them. Our bodies are "members of Christ." We belong to Him body, soul, and spirit, which makes each part of us holy. The idea of taking something holy and doing an unholy act with it—in this case, joining one's body to that of another person in an illegitimate sexual relationship—should be unthinkable to a Christian.

Paul's "Never!" in verse 15 is the strongest possible negative. It's telling us that God is anything but casual in His attitude toward the sexual behavior of His children. The reality of our responsibility to God reveals the myth of casual sex as the lie that it is.

Verse 16 presents a stunning contradiction to the idea that a person can have sex with someone whose name they might not even know and whom they may never expect to see again and then go away as if no harm was done. On the contrary, God's Word says that even illicit sex forms a bond that actually mimics the oneness of marriage.

Did you notice the marriage-type language used to describe what the world calls casual sex? The partners in a so-called one-night stand are spoken of as becoming one in body, and Paul even quoted Genesis 2:24, which is part of the first marriage ceremony, when God joined Adam and Eve and they became "one flesh."

God wants us to understand that He views sex as an expression of commitment for which the two partners are held responsible every bit as much as if they had made a commitment to each other in marriage. Each time people have sex with someone outside of marriage, when they walk away from that union they leave behind not only a part of their body but a part of their spirit as well. A part of them is torn away.

In other words, there is no such thing as casual sex. There is nothing casual about sex as God has planned and intended it. Because of the intimacy involved in sex, even with a stranger, the involvement of two people coming together has an impact upon both lives. Sex is not just another form of recreation. It is a decision that affects the whole person.

One way to bring this home to your children is to ask them if they plan to go out and get married, then divorced, then married and divorced again, and so on through a number of relationships, maybe even having a child along the way. They will almost certainly say, "Of course not." Then explain to them that this is the way God views sexual relationships, which is why sex should be reserved for marriage.

Sexual Sin Offends God by Defiling What Should Be Holy

The Scripture is clear that all sexual immorality is a defilement of the body, which is called "a temple of the Holy Spirit" in 1 Corinthians 6:19. God will not tolerate the defilement of His temple, as Jesus demonstrated when He cleansed the Jerusalem temple of merchants and others carrying on their racketeering in God's house (John 2:13-16). So we as believers, in whom the Holy Spirit lives, need to make sure that the temple of our body is clean, so that we may be a holy dwelling place for the presence of Christ.

Sexual sin defiles the body and fouls the spirit and is completely out of bounds for anyone who claims to be a follower of Jesus Christ. Parents and other adults often talk with young people about the risks of sexually transmitted diseases, and of course we should make sure that our children know the truth about the physical dangers of immorality. "The sexually immoral person sins against his own body" (1 Corinthians 6:18). Sexual sin doesn't even make sense from a human standpoint. But let's make sure to take the high road too and show our kids from God's Word the serious spiritual issues at stake in the choices they make. They need to understand that sex is sacred in God's sight, and therefore sex is far more than a chemical or hormonal reaction. It is a spiritual issue, and because this is true, the most important reason to practice sexual purity is because it is part of God's "good and acceptable and perfect" will for us (Romans 12:2).

We Should Be Our Children's Best Source for the Truth About Sex

Talking about sex usually makes parents as uncomfortable as their children, if not more so. But we can't check out on this one. The way kids react to these discussions may give you the impression that they have never talked or heard about this stuff before and that you are upsetting them by even bringing it up.

But let's get real. Even elementary-age children are talking about subjects that many of us never heard about until we were in college. If you don't talk to your kids about sex, somebody else will. Chances are, somebody else already is! And chances are, it's misguided advice from misinformed people. One of the best things you can do for your children is to make them this promise: "No matter what you hear about sex, I promise you that if you will come to me I'll tell you the truth about it."

Some parents may say, "Come on, kids aren't that naive anymore. There's so much information out there, they know what sex involves and how their bodies work. Teenagers today are better informed than a lot of adults."

Really? Then consider these two examples from a school nurse at one of the large high schools in a suburb of Dallas. When this nurse asked one young woman who came in if she was sexually active, the girl said, "No, I only have sex occasionally."

The nurse dealt with another student who was pregnant. The girl was very upset and told the nurse, "I don't know how I could be pregnant. I only had sex once!"

The safest approach to talking with your children about sex is to assume nothing in terms of their knowledge, no matter what they may say. And besides, as we pointed out before, teaching children a God-honoring approach to sex is not just a matter of helping them get their facts straight. That may be a starting point, but the spiritual side of sex is what's missing in most discussions.

———

Jack: I want to challenge fathers to step up and take the responsibility for guiding their children in this area, especially their sons. About the only advice many young men ever get from their dads is, "Don't get anybody pregnant!"

Fathers have to do a lot better job than that. We are in the best position to teach and model sexual purity to our children. Of course, this challenges us to be careful about what we allow to come into our own lives and into our homes. One dad said, "I was trying to teach my son a biblical view of sex, and then I realized that almost everything coming into my home on television contradicted everything I was trying to teach."

Dad, if that's true in your home, the answer seems like a no-brainer. Do whatever you have to do for your children's sake. We can sit in the recliner and flip the remote back and forth between games while playing armchair quarterback, but we can't play armchair father with our kids. Sexual purity is too important to hand the responsibility off to someone else.

A good place to start is by making this commitment of sexual purity for yourself: "I will not fail my Lord, my wife, my children, and my church by being unfaithful in my sexual conduct." Get your life lined up, and then be straight up and strong on this subject with your children, and one day they will thank you for it.

TEACH YOUR CHILDREN THE NECESSITY OF MODESTY

This one is worth another book. Immodesty often leads to impurity, which leads to immorality of all kinds. First Corinthians 6 ends with these words: "God bought you with a high price. So you must honor God with your body" (v. 20, NLT).

Paul also gave this instruction to the church: "I want women to be modest in their appearance. They should wear decent and appropriate clothing and not draw attention to themselves by the way they fix their hair or by wearing gold or pearls or expensive clothes. For women who claim to be devoted to God should make themselves attractive by the good things they do" (1 Timothy 2:9-10, NLT).

Be the One Who Sets the Standards for Your Children

Deb: Mothers have a huge responsibility to fulfill with their daughters when it comes to modesty in their dress and actions. Some people might say that trying to maintain modesty is one of those areas of the culture war that has already been lost. Well, it doesn't have to be lost in your house or in mine!

I'm very concerned about this not only because I raised a daughter and may have granddaughters someday but because I see immodesty creeping into the church. Some Sundays I wonder if I'm at a beach or poolside when the teenage girls pass by my pew. There seems to be little shame today, which is a good word when it is used as a synonym for modesty, the sense that certain parts of the body should not be exposed.

That's what Paul said in 1 Corinthians 12:23, which moms need to share with their daughters: "on those parts of the body that we think less honorable we bestow the greater honor, and our unpresentable parts are treated with greater modesty."

In case you're not there yet as a parent, let me assure you that most adolescent girls don't have a clue as to how the way they dress affects young men. That's why God gave girls mothers—to teach them what's appropriate and to help them dress in a way that honors God.

Sure, your daughter will face pressure from her peers at school, and maybe even at church, and she may pass that pressure along to you. For example, after a shopping trip with a teenager that became a tug-of-war over what clothes would be bought, you may start to believe there's nothing on the shelf or rack for your daughter that's decent. But that's simply not true, and we can't use it as an excuse for not standing strong. Because modesty is tied so close to purity, Jack and I both believe this is one of the biggies where we can't afford to cave in to whatever may be fashionable or popular at the moment.

Jack: Dads and sons don't get a pass on this one. The issue for men is usually not so much being modest in the way we dress—although I've had times when I was afraid a teenager was going to lose his pants coming down the aisle at church!

But we fathers have to work hard to help our sons be modest in their speech and actions. Men and boys seem to reveal their depravity most readily in "filthiness . . . foolish talk . . . crude joking" (Ephesians 5:4), none of which has a place in a Christian's life. The obvious place to start is to ask you, dad, how you talk about women and the whole issue of sexuality, and how you treat women. Your son will take his cues from you.

Dads also have a major role to play with their daughters. I have to wonder what some fathers must be thinking when they let their young daughters go out dressed provocatively. If you're uncertain about a particular piece of clothing your daughter wants to wear, try this experiment. Have her sit down, and then you sit down directly across from her. If you're shocked by what you see, then you have your call to action because whatever you see is what everybody else will see.

I'm trying to give it to you straight here. I've received letters from men of all ages who have said, "Pastor, the way some of the women at church are dressed really bothers me. I'm being tempted even at church." That breaks my heart as a pastor, but I also know that modesty or the lack thereof does not start at church. It starts in the home, which is why Deb and I want to do everything possible in this book to encourage you to fight the good fight. Our children are worth it.

Try to Lift the Discussion to a Higher Level

It's important for us as parents to take the high ground in dealing with the issue of modesty. A lot of parents get so weary wrangling about clothes that are too tight, too low, or too high that they don't have the energy left to lift the discussion to a higher level. We want to help our children view modesty as part of the larger picture of a life that is pleasing to the Lord. Since our bodies belong to Him, everything we do with them matters. A great verse to motivate your kids and to have them memorize is Colossians 3:17: "Whatever you do, in word or deed, do everything in the name of the Lord Jesus."

We don't want to pretend that it will be a cakewalk to teach your children the necessity of modesty. Our culture has become unblushable; so we can't expect to get much help out there. And our kids sometimes seem to be on the opposing side, because what every young person dreads more than anything is to be considered "different," which in youth culture is a synonym for "weird."

It's amazing today that when certain people come out of the closet and flaunt their lifestyles, they are celebrated. But if young men or women step out and say, "I'm going to be pure in my relationships and modest in the way I dress and act," they are considered weird. But it's not weird to be pure—it's wise! However, we do have to recognize that the pressure to conform is strong on our kids. And so the arguments often go something like this: "Mom, you can't be serious. *Nobody* is wearing this!" If nobody is wearing it, why is it on the market? "C'mon, Dad, the guys are going to see this movie, and they want me to go with them. I'll close my eyes during the dirty parts." If you believe that, you'll buy land in Florida without seeing it first!

What's the point? There are no magic answers that will instantly put an adolescent's mind at ease about his or her fear of being considered different. The fact is that as Christians we *are* called to look and act differently than the world. We know this as parents; the challenge is to communicate it to our kids in a way that's more subtle and effective than simply declaring loudly, "Well, you *are* different! You're a Christian!" and then cutting off the discussion.

One way you can do this is to help your children answer the question, "Who am I really trying to impress or please by the way I dress and act?" A lot of young people have never stopped to think about it or to verbalize a response, and sometimes they can arrive at the right answer themselves as we keep pointing them back to God's Word.

Another question to help your children answer is, "What are the kids really like in the circle or group I'm trying to fit into?" One dad who noticed his son wasn't hanging with the same kids anymore asked him what was up. "Aw, they're bad news" was his answer. Moments of discovery like that are priceless.

When you talk with your children you may not get the answers you were hoping for, at least not at first. But discussing things like modesty in dress and behavior with kids sure beats ragging on them all the time about their appearance and friends.

And if you want to have an interesting dinnertime discussion some evening, read Romans 13:14 and ask what Paul means by this statement: "Put on the Lord Jesus Christ, and make no provision for the flesh, to gratify its desires." Here's a cheat-sheet answer for you: the idea is that we are to be like Jesus every day in the way we look and the way we live.

A final word on modesty: think of it as a strength, not a struggle. Give your children the benefit of the doubt. Instead of cringing at the thought and tensing up, approach the issue as if you know they want to do the right thing, and make them prove otherwise. They'll appreciate you for thinking the best of them, whether they say it or not.

Putting the Plan to Work

Formulate a Plan for Victory in the Area of Sexual Purity

Victory is possible for you in the battle for the purity of your children. Here are some steps on the pathway to purity:

1. Stay involved in your children's lives, especially when they are teenagers. Keep the channels of communication open. Don't assume you can have the big sex talk once and then you're finished with it. Keep talking to your kids about their dreams and hopes and frustrations. Help them to see the big picture of life and to learn how to delay a temporary gratification now in order to gain the reward of lasting satisfaction later on.

2. Help your children understand that sex is serious. Remind them that their sexuality is a gift from God to be used in His way and for His purposes, not a toy for them to play with.

3. Help your kids see their true worth and value before God. Your children are precious in His sight. Their bodies are temples of the Holy Spirit. Don't allow your teenagers to be pressured into making poor choices because of a lack of self-esteem.

4. Remind your sons and daughters regularly that it is worth the wait to keep themselves pure until marriage. Urge them to practice abstinence, and do everything in your power to help them be morally and spiritually pure.

5. Teach your children to live with a biblical worldview. Help them learn to pass everything they see and experience through the purifying filter of God's Word.

6. Partner with your church in setting the highest possible standards for your children. Draw on the people and resources of your church to come alongside you in your desire to help your children live godly lives. Be very careful how you speak about your church in front of your children. If they sense that you do not value and esteem the church, they will follow your example and blow the church off as something not to be taken seriously.

7. Warn your young people against the consequences of sin. This is often the part we like the least. After all, it's not fun to talk with kids about things such as the higher rates of depression and suicide that occur in young people who fall into sexual sin. Your teenagers may have heard this before, along with the warnings about the incurable diseases that can come with sexual immorality. This doesn't have to be the number one item on your agenda, but don't ignore it either.

It's very possible that some of our readers are saying to themselves, "I would feel like a hypocrite if I tried to talk to my kids about sex." Perhaps you made some bad choices when you were a teenager or before you came to Christ. Or perhaps you would have to say that even though you're a Christian, you haven't really been living for Christ, and you feel as if you can't preach to your kids what you're not practicing.

We can't change the past, but we can bury it under the blood of Christ! If you need to kneel and talk to God before you stand and talk to your children, seek Him now. He has promised to forgive our sins if we confess them to Him (1 John 1:9). And by all means, if you have any doubt about your salvation, meet with your pastor or somebody who can help you. Don't let guilt over the past keep you from fighting for your kids today.

If you will honor God with your body, your mind, and your spirit, your children will rise up one day and bless you. Don't live in guilt or regret, but in the confidence and courage of a Christian parent who is dedicated to Jesus Christ.

9

BUILDING A ROCK-SOLID FAMILY

WE RECENTLY HEARD ABOUT a high-tech company in Germany with a very unusual employment policy. Workers at the Nutzwerk Company in Leipzig can actually be fired for coming to work in a bad mood! That's because of a "good mood" clause in their employment contracts that is designed to eliminate grumpiness, whining, and complaining in the workplace. Employees who wake up feeling grouchy are told to stay home and get over it rather than coming in to work.

A company spokesman said the ban on bringing a bad mood to work was made official after one employee refused to abide by Nutzwerk's philosophy of always smiling. The spokesman said this person used to complain so much that other employees started complaining about her complaining! One woman who works at the company said she really likes the "good mood" policy because this way no one can come to work in a sour frame of mind and ruin what would otherwise be a good day for everyone else.

When you read a story like that, you start to wonder what would happen if we had good mood policies in our families. No bad moods, temper tantrums, or grousing allowed. Everybody has to smile and be happy every day. Anyone who wakes up in a sour mood can't show his or her face until he or she gets over it, and whoever goes around with anything but a smile or complains about the conditions can be fired. As the kids would say, "Yeah, right. Not a chance."

We agree. Home is where it's OK to get real—and besides, you can't fire your family anyway. The reality is that everyone has a bad day now and then; so a good mood policy is actually a bad idea for a family. But that doesn't mean we have to give up on the goal of making our homes positive, encouraging, and even fun places to live. Not at all!

Now don't get the wrong idea. We're not talking about a perfect family that only exists in TV Land—you know, the *Leave It to Beaver* kind of household where Mom always wears pearls and a smile while she vacuums, and Dad is always calm and level-headed, never raising his voice, let alone his hand.

Those programs may be fun to watch and laugh with, but frankly we don't know any families like that. The image we want to give you of a solid, happy family is not from television but from God's Word. Psalm 128 describes such a family in the context of ancient Israel, particularly when families gathered together in Jerusalem to worship and celebrate during the great festivals.

Psalm 128 is a pilgrim song, which means that the throngs of Israelites who were making their way up to Jerusalem to observe the festivals would sing these songs in joyful anticipation of what awaited them. And so the psalmist wrote:

> *Blessed is everyone who fears the LORD,*
>   *who walks in his ways!*
> *You shall eat the fruit of the labor of your hands;*
>   *you shall be blessed, and it shall be well with you.*
> *Your wife will be like a fruitful vine*
>   *within your house;*
> *your children will be like olive shoots*
>   *around your table.*
> *Behold, thus shall the man be blessed*
>   *who fears the LORD. (Psalm 128:1-4)*

If you want an ideal to aim for, forget Ward, June, Wally, and the

Beav. These verses speak of a home where the father as the provider and protector is a man who walks with God and enjoys God's blessing on his work. The imagery becomes very powerful when the wife and mother is likened to "a fruitful vine" that is mature and productive, and the children are compared to little "olive shoots" that are flourishing and growing under their parents' care and provision.

These images of fruitfulness and healthy growth were very meaningful in an agricultural society that depended on vines, olive trees, and other crops for its livelihood. Describing a family in this way is the highest compliment that any home could be paid.

Our choice of words to describe a solid, happy, flourishing family would certainly be different today. But such a family has to be possible or the Scriptures would not hold it up to us as an example. We believe that a home like this is not only possible but within the reach of any family that is willing to follow the precepts of God's Word and rely on the Holy Spirit. Here are three ways you can build a rock-solid family.

ROCK-SOLID FAMILIES ARE BUILT BY LOVING TOGETHER

One prayer we had as we wrote this book is that the importance of a family's love for each other would come through loud and clear. Dad and Mom set the example for this by their love relationship. Let your children know that you love each other and love them by hugging and kissing each other and them. Kids feel a tremendous sense of security when they see that, which is why our love for each other is even more crucial to a family's health than some parents may realize.

We say this because youth experts tell us that the number one question on kids' minds today is, "Mom and Dad, are you two still in love with each other?" In other words, our children want to be reassured that they are not going to wake up one day and discover that their parents are splitting up. So don't be afraid to openly express your affection for each other in front of your children. Along with this, how can we express our love and affection for our children?

PUTTING THE PLAN TO WORK

Express Your Love by Embracing Your Children

Children need the warm, affectionate touch of their parents, and they need it at every stage of their lives. Don't ever believe that you're not supposed to hug or kiss your children as they get older. Being up front with your love is so critically important that the Bible says, "Better is open rebuke than hidden love" (Proverbs 27:5).

Jack: We fathers need to give our kids physical affection, so that they not only hear us saying we love them, but they feel loved. I can hear some dads saying, "I'm really not comfortable doing that."

Well, get over it! Those who study young people indicate that frequent hugs will actually help protect your children from moral impurity. For example, a girl who enjoys the warm, wholesome embrace of her father is far less likely to go looking for affection, affirmation, and love in all the wrong places as she grows into her adolescent and young adult years.

I have always looked to the story of the prodigal son in Luke 15 as a model for how I need to love my children. Jesus said that while this young man was far from home living in sin and humiliating himself and his family, his father stood at the door of the house every day looking for his son to come home.

I love what the prodigal's father did when he finally saw his son come into view on the horizon one day. The Bible says this dad ran to his son, then "ran and embraced him and kissed him" (v. 20). The form of the verb indicates that the father kissed his son again and again and again. That father is a picture of God the Father and His extravagant love for His children. Give your kids love by expressing affection personally and frequently to them.

Deb: It's no secret that a lot of fathers and husbands are reluctant to express affection because it makes them feel uncomfortable or awkward. A wife can really help a husband like this by patiently encouraging him to verbalize and demonstrate his affection. One way is by stepping back and letting him have more times of direct interaction with the children.

Women whose husbands aren't used to expressing affection sometimes cover for them by becoming their voice to the children. It often goes something like this: "Mommy, does Daddy really love me?" "Of course he does, dear. You know your father loves you." If your family has conversations like this, you need to help Dad learn how to communicate his love to his children.

Express Your Love by Encouraging Your Children

Children and young people need as much affirmation as they do affection. Sometimes parents feel like cheerleaders, and that's OK because they are. Conferring your blessing is a big part of this encouragement.

It's amazing how many times we hear adults say, "My father never once said he was proud of me or affirmed me in what I wanted to do." The fact that many of the people who say this are famous in some field is interesting. Many times these people were driven to excel either by the desire to win their parents' approval or because of an "I'll show you what I can do" attitude that they adopted out of anger or resentment.

Our kids need to know we are behind them, which frees them to become their own people and find their place in this world. It's so hard for some parents to let go of their dreams and ambitions for their children. But our calling as Christian parents is to help our children learn how to let Jesus live *His* life through them rather than living *our* lives through them.

Express Your Love by Equipping Your Children

One of the most demanding and exciting jobs we have as parents is to equip our children to face life as whole, successful adults. Someone has said that we are not raising children, we are raising adults.

Keeping that truth in mind will help you on those late nights when you are tired and ready for bed, but your teenager suddenly wants to talk. A big part of equipping children is simply being available to counsel them at any hour. It's usually at the most unlikely times that our kids learn the most valuable lessons because they're asking for help, not because we are lecturing them.

Of course, no child is equipped who does not know God's Word well enough to make confident decisions based on it and to wield it against the enemy in spiritual warfare. If you aren't able to give your kids a lot of this world's stuff, don't feel bad. Give them what will last forever—a faith anchored firmly in the Word.

ROCK-SOLID FAMILIES ARE BUILT BY LEARNING TOGETHER

Not only do we need to *love* together, but we also need to *learn* together if we're going to build rock-solid families. The emphasis here is on *together* because we're still learning right along with our children. And because we're still learning, we are still going to make mistakes as parents. We determined long ago that if we were going to err as parents, and we did, it wouldn't be because we had stopped learning and growing.

Try to Keep Up with What's Happening and What the Kids Are Learning

Parents have a lot to do, but we can't afford to lose touch with what's happening in the world around us and with the things our children are learning. Some of the best conversations you'll have around the dinner table are about current events or school issues, especially if you help the kids see them through the lens of a biblical worldview.

That means we need to know a lot! Maybe you heard about the little boy who was lying on the floor at his father's feet one night doing his homework while Dad read the paper. "Hey, Dad," the boy asked, "what's the capital of Montana?"

Dad looked up from his paper, thought for a minute, and said, "Gee, sorry, son. I don't know."

Things were quiet for a few minutes, and then came, "Dad, what does an adverb do?"

Dad's wheels were turning behind the paper, but to no avail. "Wow, son, it's been a long time since my high-school English. I just can't remember."

The room fell silent for a few more minutes before the next question. "Dad, how do you find the square root of a number?"

"You've really got me there. Math was not my strong suit."

"That's OK, Dad," the boy said good-naturedly. "I hope you don't mind me asking you all these questions."

"Not at all, son," the dad answered triumphantly. "How can you expect to learn anything if you don't ask questions?"

Deb: Earlier I mentioned the party that friends held for Jack and me after his election to the Southern Baptist Convention presidency. One thing Jason said that night related to this subject: "Dad was wonderful at being current with what was going on. Some parents get so removed from their kids and consumed with their jobs that they lose touch. But Dad was great at talking about current events or sports. You could talk to him about anything, and he could discuss it in depth."

Help Your Children Learn How to Grow in Their Faith

The most important kind of learning that families need is what the Bible calls "grow[ing] in the grace and knowledge of our Lord and Savior Jesus Christ" (2 Peter 3:18).

Earlier in that same book, Peter gave us some incredible building blocks for constructing rock-solid kids: "make every effort to supplement your faith with virtue, and virtue with knowledge, and knowledge with self-control, and self-control with steadfastness, and steadfastness with godliness, and godliness with brotherly affection, and brotherly affection with love" (1:5-7).

One after another, we are to add to and build upon these qualities in our lives. Faith is first because it's the foundation, the starting place.

Parents can have no greater privilege than to lead their children to faith in Christ.

Our purpose as parents is to unleash on this world a generation of young people committed to the Lord Jesus Christ. This faith should be a positive, optimistic faith that dares to dream, that strives for the best, and that trusts God no matter what—a faith that prays and expects answers. That's the kind of faith we want to cultivate in our children.

The next thing 2 Peter 1:5 tells us to add to the foundation of faith is "virtue," which is moral excellence. We want our children not just to be good kids but to be God's kids. Moral excellence means having firm standards of right and wrong and seeking the highest and best even when others are settling for something less.

Moral excellence is what the apostle Paul called us to practice when he wrote: "whatever is true, whatever is honorable, whatever is just, whatever is pure, whatever is lovely, whatever is commendable, if there is any excellence, if there is anything worthy of praise, think about these things" (Philippians 4:8).

And then we are to add to our virtue "knowledge," which is spiritual understanding, the ability to live skillfully. This includes understanding the Word and the will of God. Every child deserves a Christian education, which begins in your home.

"Self-control" is the next building block in Peter's list. One of the saddest things in the world is to see adults who have little or no self-control, whether in their appetites or their attitudes. We must help our children understand that while their appetites and ambitions are God-given, they can be tempted to satisfy them in the wrong way. Some have defined temptation as the seduction to fulfill a God-given desire in a God-forbidden way.

Our natural desires are like wild horses. There are three things you can do with a wild horse. You can kill it, let it run wild, or tame and use it for a good purpose such as getting somewhere.

As Christians we are not simply to try and kill our desires, which can't be done anyway. Nor are we to let them run wild with no bridle.

The Christian faith is a matter of bringing our desires under the control of the Holy Spirit. That demands self-control, because even though the Holy Spirit is God, He will not force us to obey.

When our children are small and growing, we have to help them learn discipline by disciplining them. But ultimately our kids must learn to discipline themselves. We used to say to the children, "You either discipline yourself, or someone else will discipline you for you."

Then the Bible says to add "steadfastness" or perseverance to our character. This is patient endurance, which is tough to learn in our instant society. We microwave our meals in minutes and text instant messages on our phones (at least the kids know how to do this!), so it's no wonder we have a generation of both adults and children who say, "I want it right now."

But the definition of the word "steadfastness" in the original language shows that patience can't be rushed. The word means "to stay under." This can refer to patience in the face of trials and problems, but also the patience to stay with a task or project until it's completed.

We were both raised to be finishers; so nothing is more disturbing than to see people quit on tasks, and even quit on a marriage or other important relationship, when the going gets a little tough. Do your children, their future spouses and children, and the world in general a huge favor by instilling in your kids a positive, can-do spirit that doesn't throw in the towel when it hits a snag. Life is full of examples of people who began well but didn't finish.

The next quality is "godliness" (2 Peter 1:6). This refers to a character of life that radiates and reflects the character of God. We must teach our children that they are under the authority of Almighty God, which won't be hard for them to accept if we teach them to love God with all of their heart.

A Sunday school teacher asked her class one day, "Why do you children love God?"

Nobody seemed to have an answer until a little boy raised his hand and said, "I don't know why I love God. I guess it just runs in my family!" Loving God ought to run in your family.

We need two more qualities as we learn with our children and as we grow in faith together. Next to the last is "brotherly affection" or brotherly kindness, which is compassion for and sensitivity to others. We live in a world of takers, but God wants us to be givers.

A father in our church takes his boys to a local rescue mission every year at the holiday season and stands beside them as they serve homeless and hurting people. Those boys are learning lessons about brotherly kindness and mercy they'll never forget.

And finally, we are to add "love" to all these other qualities. Love is the counterpart of faith and a worthy trait to close out this list from the pen of the apostle Peter. When we help our children learn all of these traits, they will be growing in their love for the Lord and for others. Help your kids understand that love is not just a noun but a verb. Love acts and gives and helps and cares.

You may be saying, "Wow, that's a tall order!" Yes, it is, and the only way to do it is with the Word of God and prayer. Here's some good advice from a rather unexpected source. Lamentations 2:19 says, "Arise, cry out in the night, at the beginning of the night watches! Pour out your heart like water before the presence of the Lord! Lift your hands to him for the lives of your children." Pour your heart out for them before God daily. Pray for God's protection and power in their lives.

ROCK-SOLID FAMILIES ARE BUILT BY LAUGHING TOGETHER

There isn't a lot that needs to be said about this one. We've said it before, but it needs to be said again. Make your home a place of laughter. Some of us are far too serious.

One teenage girl said, "I just want to say to my parents, 'Lighten up!' They're so uptight." In our generation we called that making a federal case out of everything.

We're not in the business of recommending movies, but it wouldn't hurt for you to have a couple of classic, family-friendly comedies in your home that you can watch as a family and laugh until your sides hurt.

But let us warn you—families that laugh together will attract others! Your children's friends will want to come over and join in the fun. Let 'em in! Worried about the carpet? It can be cleaned, but you'll never regret the investment you make in love and laughter. A little dirt on the floor or crumbs on the table never hurt anybody. Besides, as comedienne Phyllis Diller said, "Cleaning the house while the kids are still at home is like shoveling snow when it's still snowing."

One of the great things about opening your home and sharing the joy is that the people who come through your door enrich your family and add to the fun. It's wonderful to still have a warm relationship with our children's friends who are now young adults themselves. They don't come over and clean out the refrigerator anymore, but we cherish the memories of the times when they did.

Make your home a joyful place and your kids will not only invite their friends over to be a part of your life, but they will remember it forever. And if your home is a place where you love together, learn together, and laugh together, your kids will keep coming back.

Deb: One of the best things about our family is that we laugh a lot. We laugh about life, about circumstances, and about each other. You might say a person would have to have a healthy amount of self-esteem to make it in the Graham family. There is never a moment when an opinion good or bad is not challenged and debated. Having one child become a lawyer was no surprise. But I could pit either Kelly or Josh against Jason on any given day to debate him in open court.

Strong self-esteem has led to strong kidding. We tease each other about everything. One of the kids' favorite targets is Mom. I cannot count all the times I have been barraged with jokes about my cooking (or lack thereof), my driving, or my punctuality (which I will debate with the best of them).

Laughter is one of the bonds that hold our family together. The unwritten language of laughter speaks volumes about the closeness and high esteem we hold for each other. It's just our way of saying, "I love you" and "I treasure you."

Putting the Plan to Work

Not every family has this kind of relationship, and that's OK. Find the thread that holds your family to the light side. Nurture your children to be themselves and to accept their parents and siblings. Teach the truth that there is freedom and acceptance in your family circle. You will be rewarded for years to come if there is joy to be found in your home.

10

RAISING EAGLES

PERHAPS YOU'VE HEARD the story about a mother turkey that found an unusual egg in the barnyard one day, so she decided to sit on the egg and hatch it. Out came a baby eaglet, but the mother turkey began to raise it as one of her own there in the confines of the barnyard. One day the mother turkey saw the little eaglet looking up wistfully and longingly into the sky, watching as a beautiful and majestic eagle soared high above the barnyard. "Don't even look up there," the mother turkey said. "That's an eagle, and you're a turkey. Eagles were made to fly high, but you were made for down here. Our wings don't work, so it's no use to be wishing you could fly."

So for the rest of that eagle's life, the poor creature lived a completely earthbound existence—walking around the barnyard with its nose to the ground, scratching for kernels of corn, never trying its wings and so discovering that God made it to fly. Maybe this story is the origin for the bumper sticker that says, "It's hard to soar like an eagle when you work with a bunch of turkeys!"

If you have children at home, you have emerging eagles in your nest who need to learn how to soar the way God made them to do. And even if your nest is empty right now, chances are that it won't be that way for too long. One wag said, "Young couples don't realize that the first child can come anytime. All others take nine months."

One of the most common metaphors for the task of launching our children out of the home and into the world is that of helping them test their wings and learn to fly the way an eagle teaches its young to fly. Saying that children are made to soar like eagles doesn't mean that every child will reach the top echelons of the business or sports world (but don't tell that to a parent involved in youth sports!).

But it does mean that all children have the potential to soar high above the ordinary and the status quo and, by the grace of God, become all that He has created them to be. Learning to soar means our children will love God, possess a living and vital faith, have a heart of compassion for people, and serve their generation. It means that our children and our grandchildren will display a beautiful and powerful testimony for Christ.

Children were not made to grow up in the confines of the barnyard and live an earthbound existence. So as we close out this section of the book, we want to give you some final encouragement to make sure you are raising eagles to fly high and not turkeys to scratch around in the earth. How do we raise eagles?

HELP YOUR CHILDREN DEVELOP A HEAVENLY MIND-SET

The reason we want our children to be like eagles is because an eagle has come to represent strength and character. The fact is that an eagle is not an earthly bird. It lives and flies in the heavens, from whence it has a great viewpoint of what is happening on earth.

The Bible calls all of us to build our homes and lives not just in the heavens but in heaven. "Set your minds on things that are above, not on things that are on earth" (Colossians 3:2) ought to be a theme verse of every parent. We know that whatever we think about the most and spend most of our time on, our children will probably come to value the most too. So we need to make sure that Jesus Christ and the things of God are first in our affections before we pass our faith on to our children.

Heaven Is Where Our Strength Is Found

One of the great promises of Scripture is Isaiah 40:31, which we love and have tried to keep in the forefront of our minds as we raised our children. This verse gives us a wonderful reason to teach them to have a God-centered focus and mind-set: "They who wait for the LORD shall renew their strength; they shall mount up with wings like eagles."

━━━━━

Jack: When Jason was born in 1973, I remember how shaken I was by the thought of the responsibility I had now that I was a father. I was only twenty-three years old at the time, and I can tell you that the prospect of fatherhood was scary. And when Kelly and Josh were born, some of those same feelings emerged because Deb and I took our calling as parents very seriously.

We had committed our lives to each other and to the Lord, and as our family grew we committed each child to Jesus Christ. We made mistakes along the way, but by the grace of God we have three outstanding young eagles today who are walking in the truth, who love God and their family, and who love people and have compassion for the world.

I don't consider myself to be an expert on parenting. But as I look back, I can say that every courageous decision that parents make on behalf of their children is worth the effort. Maybe for you a courageous decision would be to decide as a couple that you will live on one income, whatever that takes, and not pursue two careers while putting your children into someone else's hands to raise.

I'm glad that Deb and I determined from day one that our children would be the priority of our lives. Parents only have the stewardship of their children for a very brief season. I know that for Deb and me, the time we had to raise eagles—from Panola Street in Fort Worth where Jason was born to Josh's graduation from college and entry into the adult world—was far too valuable and far too short to waste the opportunity to love, teach, nurture, and prepare them for the world and the challenges of these times.

Putting the Plan to Work

It takes courageous parents to raise children today because there is an onslaught being unleashed against the family. It seems that every advocacy group imaginable wants to set the agenda for our children and families—from feminists and homosexual rights activists to groups like the ACLU that want to purge every vestige of religion from public life. Every day we are being bombarded by efforts to change the foundational nature of the family and restructure society. Sometimes it makes us parents wish we could just take our children home and close the door to the outside world.

But we know that if we are going to raise kids who soar as eagles, we can't protect them from all the storms. However, we can shelter them *in* the storms until they are ready to face the world as young adults.

When Jason and Kelly were small, we served at the First Baptist Church of Hobart, Oklahoma. That area in southwestern Oklahoma is known for its tremendous storms. We even had a storm cellar in the backyard of the parsonage. We well remember those times when the warning sirens would go off and we would gather the kids up to head to the storm cellar until the storm had passed over.

Those times of sheltering our children are so important. But it's even more reassuring to know that when the time comes to nudge your young eagles out of the nest and into the world, they can weather the storms because their eyes and their hopes are fixed on heaven. As a matter of fact, we are told that eagles actually fly the highest during a storm. It's as though the strong winds lift the eagle to a higher level instead of pushing him down to crash into the ground. We pray that our children will fly even higher in the days ahead as the cultural storms of this new century come against them.

Your Children Will Soar Higher If They Have Your Example to Follow

Whenever we talk about the need for Christians to be heavenly-minded, someone will usually say, "Well, you don't want people who are so heavenly-minded they're no earthly good." And someone else will often come back with the rejoinder, "The problem is that most Christians are so earthly-minded, they're no heavenly good."

There's no reason to go to either extreme. But if we had to choose as parents, we would rather have children whose minds and hearts are set on things above rather than on the things of this world. But it has to start with us, and if you're a parent you have already discovered that few things in life will test and reveal the depth of your walk with Christ like raising children.

The fact is that all things being equal, the God whom our children come to know and follow will be just as big or small as the God we serve. Children who soar are those who believe in a great God who can do the impossible and who is completely faithful and trustworthy. If you want your kids to become eagles, you have to have that kind of faith yourself so you can take them into the heavenly realms and release them there to discover the joys and challenges of living for Christ.

That's how real eagles do it. When the little eagles are ready for flight training, their mother puts them on her wings and takes them into the sky. At just the right moment, the mother eagle swoops out from under her baby, leaving it to fly alone. And if the eaglet starts to plunge, the mother swoops back and catches it. This training regimen goes on as many times as necessary until the baby eagle finally gets its wings and is able to soar on its own.

The problem with parents who are spiritually earthbound is that they can't take their kids into the heavens, even though that's what their kids are made for and are longing for.

Maybe you're saying at this point, "Isn't there any part of parenting that doesn't involve me having to get my act together first?"

If there is, we haven't discovered it. Take heart, though, because we don't have to be perfect to be parents. But we should at least be growing in our faith and in the knowledge of Christ (2 Peter 3:18).

Here's a great verse to encourage as you seek to raise eagles who will soar high for the Lord. We serve a God "who is able to do far more abundantly than all that we ask or think" (Ephesians 3:20). Claim that power for yourself, give your kids an unshakable faith in our great God, and they'll fly straight up.

LET YOUR CHILDREN KNOW YOU EXPECT GREAT THINGS FROM THEM

If you expect minimum results with your children, that's exactly what you'll get. We always tried to set high standards for our children, not to pressure or exasperate them, but to encourage them to do their best.

Make Sure Your Expectations Are Realistic

There is a fine line between having high expectations and demanding more of children than they can do, but parents who really study and know their children can usually discern the difference.

For instance, a child who has good intellectual capacity but brings home a string of D's on his or her report card needs to be challenged to do better. But listen to the difference between the following two approaches.

Approach 1: "Son, it's pretty obvious you aren't trying because I know you can do better. What's the problem?"

Approach 2: "What's wrong with you? You're embarrassing our family. Your sister hasn't gotten anything but A's since she was in school, and we expect the same thing out of you. You're grounded until you turn every one of those D's into an A!"

The problem with approach two is that B's may be the extent of this son's ability. But in any case it's irrelevant what his sister is capable of. Putting him on a performance basis with her as the standard is destined to lead to frustration and possible rebellion on his part.

But when all is said and done, we need to hold the standards high for our children. We used to say to our children, "'I can' will beat 'I can't' every single time." In fact, our kids learned that "I can't" was in most cases not an appropriate response in our household. The reason was that "I can't" usually meant "I don't want to." We wanted our kids to know they *could* because as Christians they were able to say, "I can do all things through [Christ] who strengthens me" (Philippians 4:13).

Teach Your Children to Rise Above the Crowd

Expecting great things from our children is so important in the spiritual realm. One of the most important "great things" they will need to learn in the world they face is having the courage to rise above the crowd and to stand for the Lord even if no one else joins them.

The great prophet Daniel and his friends—Shadrach, Meshach, and Abednego—are shining biblical examples of this ability. They were taken into captivity from Israel to Babylon when they were just teenagers (Daniel 1). They were put under extreme pressure to conform to Babylonian society and to worship Babylonian gods. But they refused to compromise their convictions even when they were far from home and could have rationalized that they were under a death threat if they didn't give in.

We don't know anything about the families of Daniel and his buddies. But there must have been four sets of parents back in Israel who raised eagles because these guys soared far above the crowd. Other Hebrew captives were taken with them, but we have to assume from the story that those other young men yielded to the pressure and became Babylonian in their tastes, habits, and worship.

The pressure on our kids to conform is enormous, and it starts a lot earlier than it did when we were in school. The major reason kids try alcohol, drugs, and sex is because of peer pressure, the desire to please or impress their friends. But we know that if our children hang with the wrong crowd, they will soon become the wrong kind of person.

God's Word has some strong warnings for us on this one. "Do not be deceived: 'Bad company ruins good morals'" (1 Corinthians 15:33). "The companion of fools will suffer harm" (Proverbs 13:20). This is why it is important for us to help our children choose the right friends. It's our responsibility to help them choose the people they know and the places they go.

The question often comes up at this point, "But aren't we as Christians supposed to be making friends with unbelievers so we can share Christ with them and influence them for Him?"

Of course we are. But the problem in a lot of these relationships is that the influence is flowing in the wrong direction. There's no question that we want our children to care about reaching unbelievers and to actively share their faith. But a lot of children, especially in the preteen and early teenage years, don't yet have the discernment to make those crucial distinctions and are vulnerable to the wrong influences. That's why our involvement has to be strong at first before we can begin to back off and let our children make more and more of their relationship and other decisions.

And don't forget to make use of the other mentors God puts in your children's lives. We've talked a lot about the church's crucial role in the family, but your kids' school also has people who can have a very positive and lasting impact. We usually only hear about the bad cases and the instances when the influence is negative, but all of us can remember teachers and coaches who influenced us in the right way and impacted our lives.

This means it's as important to know your children's teachers and other adults who have influence over them as it is to know their friends. It's not likely that all of the teachers and administrators in your child's school will share your faith, unless you are in a Christian school. But whichever kind of school your children attend, they still need to learn how to soar above the crowd and to stand strong for the Lord, even if it means standing alone.

HELP YOUR CHILDREN TO EMBRACE THE PRESENCE AND POWER OF CHRIST

Here is Isaiah 40:31 again: "they who wait for the LORD shall renew their strength; they shall mount up with wings like eagles." The only way we can wait upon the Lord is to spend time in His presence. And the ones who live in His presence are the ones who discover His great power that makes them soar.

Sometimes young people who are in the full bloom of their youth and strength feel as if they don't need as much buoying up as us old-timers. But we know better, because needing the presence and power of Jesus Christ has nothing to do with age.

In fact, there's a very interesting statement just before verse 31 of Isaiah 40: "Even youths shall faint and be weary, and young men shall fall exhausted" (v. 30). Parents often envy the youth and energy of their children, but the truth is that none of us can make it on our own. If you can communicate to your children the need and the *joy* of cultivating the presence of Christ, they'll discover a power that sustains them when even youthful vigor has failed.

So be faithful in raising those eagles. And if they are about ready to fly the nest, or have already flown, keep praying for them. One parent said, "Well, my children are gone now. So I guess all I can do is pray for them." That's the *best* thing you can do for your children, no matter what their age! And as you pray for your children, you also will soar into the heavenly realms where God's presence is real and where your own strength will be renewed.

We never really owned our children. They belong to God. And so even before they were born, we gave them to Him. And when it came time to let them fly into the future that God had planned for them, we let go and have been watching God work in their lives. So our encouragement to you is this: be courageous parents, and let your children go so they can fly high to the glory of God.

PART THREE

Special Reflections
from Deb Graham

11

FROM "IT'S A BOY" TO "I'M ENGAGED"

JACK: I ASKED FOR THE PRIVILEGE of introducing these two chapters from Deb's pen and heart. She is the light and joy of my life, my best friend and companion through life whose love and commitment have been the strength beneath me in our ministry together. Besides this, Deb has always been the heart and soul of our family and has made our home the special place it was for our children, and still is today. As a mother and wife Deb is the best in my book, and I want to express my love and admiration for the wonderful person she is.

I'm glad that Deb has this opportunity to share some thoughts from her heart as she reflects on the incredible joy and adventure we have had together of being parents. I've been the beneficiary of her wisdom and insights for over thirty years now, and I feel honored to recommend that you give these chapters a careful and prayerful reading. You'll find a lot of seasoned counsel from a mom who has been there and did the job and continues to bless her family and everyone who knows her with her love for the Lord and for others.

It is probably not the best idea to start your morning out with cable news programs. But Jack and I really enjoy one early-morning news program whose hosts have become so familiar to us, you could almost say they are our "friends."

One particular morning we woke up early as usual, and the ritual began. Jack has to have his coffee, so he made his way to the kitchen and waited patiently while his favorite blend dripped to perfection. I don't drink coffee but prefer my caffeine in a glass with ice and fizz.

But on that morning my Dr. Pepper had barely finished its fizz over the ice when our favorite news program suddenly became anything but routine. The usual Los Angeles car chase report was over, with the police winning again. As the program retuned to the next news story, my attention was grabbed by the story of a woman in Colorado who had admitted to having sex parties for high-school boys and having sex with several of them. She pleaded guilty to sexual assault charges. The authorities said she had also supplied drugs and alcohol to the teens. The detective on the case said the woman described herself as a "cool mom" who was never popular in high school and only was beginning to feel like "one of the group."

As I tried to take in the horror of this story, I stopped drying my hair and stood riveted in front of the television, waiting to see this woman. I was surprised to see that she looked very normal, with a stylish haircut and average looks. Somehow I wanted her to look devilish and repulsive, which would have made the story easier to swallow.

Actually that was a hard story to take anyway. I couldn't help but wonder what in the world is happening to parents today who seem to have completely lost sight of their responsibility to protect and train and nurture their children to healthy maturity. Sure, "sex party mom" is an extreme case, but she is only at the far end of a continuum that reaches all the way from great parents to "what in the world are they thinking?" parents.

PARENTING IS A LIFELONG CALLING

From the moment the pregnancy test confirms that you are going to be a parent, you enter the first stages of what will become a reality for the rest of your life. Many parents think their job is done the moment their child reaches eighteen or twenty-one, but whoever said that parenting comes with an expiration date? I do not believe this is what the Bible teaches or that God our Father turns us over to ourselves and checks out when we reach a certain age.

In fact, I have discovered that the opposite is true. The older I get, the more dependent I am upon my heavenly Father. With age I need His guidance and wisdom more and more in my life and long to be with Him more often. Someday I will find complete happiness when I can sit at His feet and worship Him for all eternity.

So don't tell me that a parent's job is over when his or her children reach adulthood. Being a parent is a lot like being married. You are committed to be there in sickness or in health, for richer or poorer, till death do you part. And even after death, a parent's skills or lack thereof continue to influence future generations.

But there are different and distinct seasons of parenting, just as there are seasons of life. The problem in America is that many parents grow frustrated or disillusioned in one season and never move on to the next one. The challenge we face is to learn to trust God in each season, and the joy is to see Him equip us in unique ways for each unique season.

Today's young families have more books, CDs, DVDs, self-help programs, and other materials available on the subject of parenting than any previous generation. Yet, while we are giving our children input to make them Baby Einsteins, we are breeding ignorance of the Bible. We are technology-savvy but out of touch on how to pray. We are leaving a legacy of tolerance but are leaving a void in the understanding of truth and its power. In reality, we don't seem to be getting any better at being parents.

So what can we do? How can we succeed at the most cherished calling anyone can have? To meet the challenges, we must be armed with every weapon that God has available for us. We must be smarter than the devil and protected by the Holy Spirit. We must be committed for a lifetime of service, knowing that it will cost us our freedom, leisure time, money, and tears to be good parents, but that it is worth every sacrifice.

To understand how to parent, we need to examine the seasons of being a parent and how we best can use our skills in each season.

THE SEASON OF PROTECTION

Sometimes we older parents forget how helpless a baby is, how completely dependent on us for everything. It wasn't until our grandson was born that I remembered just how fragile babies really are.

As I think back to the early years, it was almost like having a new doll when my first child was born. Most of the time I was so tired I was just happy if I could make it through the day until Daddy came home. I picked out the clothes, made bottles, changed diapers, and so on every day. New moms eventually find their routine, and calm comes to the home. Then it dawns on you one day when you are rocking that little bundle that he's depending on you for everything.

I remember the night when Jason was just a few weeks old. I sat in the dark and rocked for over an hour because I just couldn't bear to put him down. I rocked, sang, and cried because I couldn't believe God would entrust me with such a perfect baby. Little did I know then that before too long I would rock and cry and ask God where that sweet, perfect little baby went as my toddler learned to say "No!" and wore me out!

The precious first years of a child's life are a season of protection. First, it's cradling their soft little heads, making sure they are properly supported. Then it's placing them to sleep in the proper position and keeping the air bubbles out of their bottles. On and on the precautions go, until the magic day that they turn over and begin to crawl.

You know at that time those first steps can't be far away, and suddenly they can walk. It's exciting, but now you have a house full of hazards from which to protect your children. How is it that they find every electric plug and every piece of lint on your spotless floors and leave their fingerprints on every mirror in the house? But protection is your game, and it's a full-time job.

I want you to know those instincts are still there. Recently I sat on a couch in the lobby of a restaurant, waiting for my daughter Kelly to join me. Seated next to me was a young man holding a tiny baby. I struck up a conversation and asked him the baby's name and age. He became very animated and told me the details as he began to bounce the baby around. But he was not being careful to cradle the baby's head, and I almost had a panic attack. Just as I was figuring out how I could get that infant out of his arms, the mother appeared and took the baby. I breathed a sigh of relief, and during the meal I kept glancing over at this young family's table to make sure that the father was not holding the baby.

Once a protective parent, always a protective parent, I guess. I think the instincts are always with us because God gave them to us to protect our children.

Years ago we lived in Fort Worth while Jack was attending seminary. We were privileged at that time for Jack to be the assistant pastor at his home church, Sagamore Hill Baptist Church. With this position we were provided with a lovely, two-bedroom home just a block from the church. Our oldest, Jason, was born while we were living there.

Jason was always aggressive and ahead of the scale on the motor charts. So when he walked at eight and a half months, we were so excited. He loved to go walking all around the house and especially loved trying to maneuver the step down into our family room. He became quite good at holding on to the wall to balance himself as he took that one step down.

After Jason had been walking for about a month, his grandmother bought him a brand-new pair of blue walking shoes. They were beautiful. We purchased an Easter outfit to go with the shoes and were all set for the debut of his "big boy" shoes at church. That morning Jack and Jason were dressed and ready to go to church. Jack decided to take Jason outside and let him walk up and down the sidewalk so Mom could have a few minutes to get ready.

Jack held out his hand and let Jason hold onto his finger to make sure he stayed on the sidewalk. It was a precious sight, our little strawberry-blond toddler and his doting dad out for a walk. But soon Jason, being the independent child that he was, didn't want to have to hold Dad's hand. And Jack, being the kind of father that he is, decided to let Jason have a little freedom.

So Jason took off, but neither he nor Jack was prepared for the fact that the sidewalk had cracks. Those beautiful blue shoes caught on a piece of the cracked, uneven pavement, and little Jason went down hard. Jack quickly bent down to pick up Jason, who was bawling so loudly, the entire neighborhood could hear. His knees were bloody and his shoes scraped.

Jason may have been in physical pain, but Jack was in heart pain because he had to bring Jason in to face me, and I would not be happy. I will never forget the scene as the front door swung open and my eyes moved from the bloody knees to the weepy eyes of one distressed dad.

Jack's only words were, "I shouldn't have let go of his hand." And from that day on, I don't think I ever saw Jack let go of any of the kids' hands. Not when they were toddlers, teenagers, or young adults, and not now that we are grandparents. He may not physically be holding on, but he holds on with hands of prayer.

The season of protection is precious. It is a learning time, and now that it is past for us as far as our children are concerned, it seems like it was far too short.

THE SEASON OF PREPARATION

The ringing of that first school bell is a perfect symbol of the change in the seasons of parenting from protection to preparation. That bell starts a race that you and your children will run for what seems like forever as you give them up to the school every morning and reclaim them every afternoon. Your children will change while they are away from you, and it is your job to mold them to what God intends for them to be.

I never cried when my children started first grade. It was when I left them at college that my world collapsed. I will never forget when we took Kelly, our daughter, to college. We loaded all of our cars and headed out for the long trip to an adjacent state. Arriving on campus we experienced all the "freshman parent" activities. I remember sitting in the school chapel that late summer morning and envisioning her singing in the university musical. I knew that her chosen field of voice would be challenging but that she would rise to the occasion.

As any parent of a freshman student can attest, the move-in is extremely painful. And I mean that both emotionally and physically. We were elated to find that her room was on the first floor! After hours had passed, Jack had to leave us to travel to a speaking engagement. His good-bye was sweet and quick. Kelly and I still had errands to run and last-minute touches to make the transformed room complete.

The next morning it was my time to say good-bye. I put up a brave front until I turned out of the parking lot and glanced back for one last wave. Then from nowhere came floods of tears and emotions, which I could not comprehend. The trip back took only four hours, but it was years in emotional time. My little girl, my best friend, my baby, was hundreds of miles away, but more than that her room at home was empty. No more fixing meals together, no more shopping, no more girl talk late at night. She was growing up, and I was a basket case! I had the hardest time when I did not have the daily opportunity to look into my kids' eyes and see what was lying beneath. Were they happy? Were they healthy? And most importantly, were they holy?

During the school years a deeper relationship is formed between parent and child. Protection is still a part of the equation, but there is so much more. A bonding takes place as each child discovers his or her place in the family. The preparation years need to be a period of exploration, acceptance, love, and fun.

The Lord knows that we made mistakes as parents, but we sure did have fun! Our children got to go to denominational and other church-related conventions, and we had some great family vacations. We decorated for each holiday, celebrated lavishly for birthdays, played ball in the house, and had lots of kisses and hugs. As the children grew older, we traveled overseas and learned to ski together. We played games and ate lots of fast food. We had a normal family life even inside the "fishbowl" of a pastor's home.

One event that stands out in my memory is Family Night. The years we spent in Florida were especially fun since the children ranged in age from birth to ten. The master bedroom in our home was on the second floor over the garage. Every night the kids begged not to have to go down to their bedrooms, which were down the stairs and across the house from ours.

So we finally agreed that Friday night would be Family Night, which included either pizza or going out to eat, watching a movie together, and the kids getting to bring their bedrolls up to our room to spend the night. It would always end up with a wrestling match on our king-size bed with Kelly crying from the effects of her brothers' roughhousing. Mom would always have to break it up, and Josh would end up sleeping in the bed with us. How I wish for those days again!

But I was snapped back to reality the eventful day that Jason confirmed what we had seen coming for some time: he wanted to ask Toby, the love of his life, to marry him. The journey from the delivery room where the doctor announced, "It's a boy" to the day when Jason got engaged suddenly seemed very brief.

12

FROM "I DO" TO "WHEN WE ALL GET TO HEAVEN"

I WILL NEVER FORGET the swirl of emotions that surrounded the engagement and marriage of Jason and Toby, the wonderful young woman we call our daughter-in-love.

THE SEASON OF PARTNERING

Like most parents of newlyweds, I really didn't know what this season of parenting would involve. Somehow I believed the myth that once my children found a mate, my job would be over. But I am discovering that as challenging as the seasons of protection and preparation are, the season of partnering is a whole new learning experience.

With the "I do" that your child says come a lot of "I don'ts" on a parent's part. I don't know what to do. I don't know how to act. I don't know what to say. I care and love more than I ever have, but I know there are two women in Jason's life while there was one before. And I didn't know exactly how to handle this as a mother. But I'm learning and having a great time at it (good thing, because it will happen again when Josh marries). And I can't even begin to imagine what it will be like to help Jack give Kelly away. Jack likes the line that for a father, giving your daughter in marriage to a young man is like giving a priceless Stradivarius violin to a gorilla.

SPECIAL REFLECTIONS

I am convinced that most parents believe that when their child marries, the new spouse will simply become a new addition to the family and everything will go on pretty much as it has in the past, only with one more person to share the family fun. And, of course, the new couple will always spend Thanksgiving and Christmas at your house. It's kind of like having your child's best friend come over for a fun time, only on a more permanent basis.

I think I shared that myth, but I was in for a big surprise. Even if you are as blessed as we are to have a dream of a mate for your child, life changes dramatically in the season of partnering as parents are required to take on an entirely different role. Sometimes you will be part of their lives, and other times you will just be an observer. But at all times you become their partner.

When Jason was seriously dating Toby, who is now his wife, he was in law school and already away from home except for holidays. We often felt we were in the dark concerning his life. Just who was this woman who wanted to date our son? Why did he want to be with her instead of coming to Family Night? And why was he so serious all the time?

I'll never forget the first time the rest of the Graham family met Toby. It was at a restaurant over dinner, and I had threatened Kelly and Josh to behave so we could try to appear as a normal family. That's not always easy for a pastor's family since people tend to have the idea that pastors and their families must sit around at home in choir robes having Bible studies. But as Kelly said, "If people only knew how normal our family is, they would be shocked."

We all arrived at the restaurant, and to say the least we were excited. So I know we came across as extremely giddy and talkative. Toby looked like she was overwhelmed. We were all talking at once, firing questions back and forth and teasing each other as we downed the food. I remember at one point in the evening Toby excused herself to go to the restroom, and I followed, praying she wasn't going to throw up.

She didn't and not only survived that first meeting but has become quite adept at taking care of herself at family gatherings. This means being able to dish it out because survival of the fittest is important in our family.

The first years of marriage are a separation from family. It's a time for the newlyweds to become one in soul and spirit. They need a lot of time to themselves and plenty of space to explore their relationship. This is a necessary process, but it's still hard to give your child who was once so dependent on you to another. This season is not the end of the parenting role, however. It is just a new assignment.

It was something of a shock to discover that my child had grown to be a man. Jason had the responsibility of a wife, a home, law school, and a job. He didn't have time to tell Mom all the details anymore. Everything was "fine" because Mom and Dad didn't need to know everything. There were also times of getting acquainted because now there was also another set of parents to consider. We are doubly blessed in that area, for Toby comes from a wonderful family.

I also discovered a new sense of loneliness during this time. We were still enjoying Kelly and Josh at home, but one chair was empty at the family table.

One challenge for parents in the season of partnering is that more often than not, you become a silent partner in the lives of the new couple. You are always there if needed, but you need to wait to be asked for advice or help. I prayed for Jason every day as I always had. I asked God to make him patient, loving, and strong. I wasn't always aware of how my prayers were being answered, but I prayed. And I focused more on the other two who were still in the preparation years, while trying to keep the newlyweds informed and included.

Still, to only see your children from a distance is to lose something of the spark you feel when you live together. This period of adjustment can be difficult and emotional, but it certainly doesn't mean that family fades from the picture.

The Scripture declares that a man is to leave his father and mother and cleave to his wife (Genesis 2:24), but it never says that the family is to leave the couple. Many of the young couples I am around today crave their families' concern, love, and guidance. We do young couples a disservice to assume that they have all the answers and don't need or want to hear from us. Everybody needs a partner and friend.

God gave me a person like this years ago when we were called to the church in Oklahoma. The church was full of wheat farmers, many of German descent, wonderful people who took on the job of mentoring a dynamic young pastor, his wife, and their two-year-old son.

I quickly fell in love with the people and my new home. This was our first pastorate, and I wanted it to be successful. I wanted the church and Jack to be proud of me, so I decided that I would be the first perfect pastor's wife. I joined the choir, taught a junior high Sunday school class, played piano for the youth choir, and helped Jack with whatever he needed. I awoke every morning and hurriedly dressed. I wanted to make sure that if anyone dropped by the parsonage they would find me dressed, the house clean, and my child perfectly behaved.

Not long after we arrived, the voice teacher at the local high school quit just before the new school year was about to start. The next Sunday morning I sang a solo in the service and filled in at the piano. Afterward the superintendent of schools asked to speak to me and offered me the voice teacher's job. He said they needed someone desperately and would look for a permanent teacher during the semester if I could get them started. I was very flattered. Although I had a minor in music in college, I had never taught school. After talking it over with Jack, I accepted the position.

I must have been crazy. Basically, what I had agreed to do was baby-sit the school's football team. I had the same group of boys (with a few cheerleaders mixed in) for music, science, history, and homeroom. Yes, I wound up trying to teach all those subjects. And to top it all off, I found out a few weeks into the job that I was pregnant.

Life was not happy in our beautiful little parsonage. I was tired, stubborn, overworked, and overcommitted at church and began throwing up. This lasted for a few weeks until one Sunday morning I ran out to the dryer to throw a load of clothes in before church and started miscarrying. Lying in a hospital room making out my final exams was not my idea of being the perfect pastor's wife.

Thankfully, God had a partner there for me—a woman who was a few years older than me. She helped with Jason and with things around the house, but more importantly she let me know that I didn't have any-thing to prove. She said I didn't owe the church, the school, or the town anything, but I did owe my family something.

To this day I remember the friendship this woman offered a young wife and mother. I needed her prayers and her quiet, calming spirit. She didn't lecture; she just enjoyed being with me, and I with her. It hasn't been until later in our ministry that I have been able to live in the same town as my mother, but God always provided Jack and me with people who became parent figures to us. Some may not have realized their influ-ence, but their mark is on our lives just as surely as if they had been our natural parents.

THE SEASON OF PRIVILEGE

The aging process is gradual and always appears to be just over the hori-zon—until you write your birth date on a form you are filling out and stop to add up the years!

Life has definitely thrown us some curves along the way. The sum-mer we were married, Jack lost his father to a violent crime. It wasn't long before his mother developed a heart problem as living alone took its toll.

Just a short time after we lost Jack's father, my dad was diagnosed with cancer and only survived a few months. He died in his mid-forties, leaving a young wife and my sister in high school. We would once again face tragedy a few years later when Jack's mom died. Jack says she died of a broken heart. We were young, grieving, and trying to console our remaining parent, my mother.

Looking back now, we know that God was and still is in control. We grew up fast, and we were able to meet people in pain at their level. Jack and I strongly believe that the death of three of our parents molded our way of parenting in an extraordinary way.

Being in the ministry meant that we led very public lives, but we molded a very private family. Through the years we have expanded our family to include fellow ministry staff and friends who have blessed us with their love and loyalty. Our children look upon these people as family. We fellowship together, pray together, and sometimes cry together.

God gave us back many times over the relationships that we needed to help fill the void left by the early deaths of our parents. Older friends provided us with unconditional love and an example of solid marriages and families. Even though Jack and I have been married for over thirty-five years, we still appreciate and look to those older than us as a pattern for our lives.

Though life dealt a cruel blow to my young, widowed mother, God in his grace led her to a wonderful man to care for her and share the same values I was raised with. Mom has experienced the joy of grandchildren and now a great-grandchild. Her energy and boundless love of life amazes me. She practices the discipline of happiness with a glow that few women can match.

Mom prays faithfully for her family. She serves endlessly in volunteer opportunities at our church. And there is always a baked treat to reward staff members or a note of encouragement. Mom's life is blessed because she chose to turn heartache into purpose. She is building a legacy of aging with grace that I want to emulate in my life. I want my children to remember that they come from a long line of people who love the Lord, love them, and seek to love others.

SUMMING IT ALL UP

The times of protecting, preparing, partnering, and privilege that we have as parents happens fluidly. One moment you hold that tiny little hand, and it seems in the next moment that hand is holding the hand of the person your child has chosen for life. Whatever season you are in as a parent, cherish it. Just don't try to hold on to it forever.

There are times when I am alone that I miss my dad. Although it has been many years since he left us, I sometimes am reminded of him in endearing ways. Every time I smell Fritos, I see him driving in his pickup delivering mail on his rural route. A bag of Fritos are open on the seat beside him, and he is humming his way through the back country roads.

Sometimes when I look at Jason and he turns his head to speak to me, I see a glimpse of my dad, whom our kids never got to know. And every time I hear the song "When We All Get to Heaven," I see Dad— lying in pain in a hospital bed, unaware of his surroundings, but teaching his boys' Sunday school class and leading them in that song. These are visions of a legacy that I want desperately to impart to my children.

I feel a burden for today's families to experience that kind of love. But too often children are experiencing fatigue, frustration, and loneliness. We have latch-key kids, absent fathers, peer pressure, and "cool moms" trying to find acceptance from their children in destructive ways.

But take heart, my fellow parent. There is a God who still reigns, and there is a Manual for every season of life. The Bible is still our authority, and its promises are as true today as ever. We must not give up our children to those who would turn their minds and hearts away from the Lord. During the season of preparation, let's commit ourselves to raise godly men and women. The future of our families, and indeed of our nation, rests in our doing the job—and we can do it in the strength that God provides.

Courageous parenting? Yes, but much more—courageous living.

IMPORTANT VOICES

Many voices are crying out to parents today. The world loudly broadcasts its call to be tolerant, compromising, and indifferent. But there are other words that I long to hear, and those are the ones I take heart from today. Truth still calls out to parents. It can be heard if we listen carefully to those who want the best for our homes.

First, I am still listening to how God speaks concerning my family. I am His child, and He still wants the home to be His training ground for our families. I am more dependent on Him than ever before. His words still provide me with wisdom and understanding.

I am dependent as never before on my helpmate and partner, Jack. We are a team continually working on our game plan. We still pray, study, and talk about our preaching skills. Each new stage brings us to a deeper realization of how much we need each other and the Lord.

Then there are four very important voices that speak so loudly that sometimes I shudder to realize the wealth of their words, for our children without realizing it are writing the real parenting manual. Every day they speak volumes of what I need to hear.

All parents reap what they sow in their children's lives. Some children express their needs early in life, others more subtly later in age. Many times the appeal is made verbally. In our case this may occur at family celebrations, at other times in a card or note given on special occasions.

I am a card saver. I have kept all the Valentine, birthday, and Mother's Day cards that my children have given me over the years. I have discovered that when pushed to put their affection into words, our children are honest and straightforward. The card may be commercial, but the written notes are priceless.

If we have learned anything from our children, we can without hesitation say that they needed security. In every word, deed, or gesture they absorbed from us what they needed most—acceptance. We only have to listen to hear their needs. For over thirty years now we have listened and have found the following to be true in our children's lives.

• 1) Our children needed to have parents that were real. They wanted to see their father be exactly who he claimed to be and do exactly as he said he would do. They expected their mother to be loyal and supportive of their father in everything he set out to do.

• 2) Our children needed the assurance that their parents were totally committed to each other and that their home was a place of love and stability.

• 3) Our children needed their home to be a haven of acceptance and understanding in the midst of an uncertain world. They wanted to be able to share their home with their friends.

• 4) Our children needed the unconditional acceptance of who they were regardless of their physical appearance, intelligence, or personality.

• 5) Our children needed and wanted to be involved in their parents' lives. They wanted special events in our home, vacations, and other outings. They desired to be involved and accepted by our friends.

• 6) Our children wanted to see faith and love in action, and not just talk.

• 7) Our children needed to see that commitment is the bond that holds everything together including marriage, home, and relationships. They wanted to see and understand sacrifice and to see value placed upon self-denial.

• 8) Our children needed to see their parents accept responsibility for their mistakes and to ask forgiveness when we wronged each other.

• 9) Our children needed to see their parents verbally express their reliance upon God for guidance in all areas of life.

• 10) Our children needed to know that their parents would never abandon them, stop loving them, or cease praying for them as long as they lived.

No child psychologist could have stated the needs of a child more profoundly than have our four by their actions and expressions of love. When time plays out its final judgment on how successful we were as parents, we will claim the promise found in Proverbs 22:6(NKJV): "Train up a child in the way he should go, and when he is old he will not depart from it."

A MAN OF GOD
Jack Graham

Pastor Jack Graham highlights what he believes it takes to be a man—specifically, to be a man of God. This book is filled with solid biblical counsel for men in personal and group study.

HC 1-58134-662-X   **$17.99**